D1125870

Tomorrow's
CIO

Strategic Executive Conversations

ASHWIN RANGAN

TOMORROW'S CIO: Strategic Executive
Conversations

©2008 by Ashwin Rangan This edition
published by The Insightful Group.

For information address The Insightful Group,
Palo Alto, CA

First Edition
ISBN-13: 978-0-692-00101-1

Library of Congress PCN: 2008943909

ISBN-13: 978-0-692-00101-1(hardbound : alk.
paper)

Printed in the United States of America

Tomorrow's
CIO

Strategic Executive Conversations

ASHWIN RANGAN

Foreword by: Rob Carter

In my professional life, I have always been an "IT guy." Having graduated with a degree in computer and information sciences, I busily set about programming solutions to business problems. Notice that I did not say that I busily set about programming a DEC Vax, or an IBM mainframe or an HP mini-computer. Although that would have been a true statement, it would not have captured the true intent of the work that has become my life's calling. It has always been about the business.

After a couple of years living in the trenches of technology, I began to work more and more closely with my business partners. I loved the technologies that improved their productivity and drove their decision making. I worked with executives and analysts alike to empower them with a new class of tools that allowed them to write their own queries and build their own spreadsheets. I worked with them to satisfy their need to get access to the information that was locked away in the machines we all identified with.

I have found that strategic conversations were in fact the key to successfully delivering on the promise of a future rich in information.

Strategic relationships with the business enabled an intriguing future where businesses connected with their workers, customers and suppliers through the strategic application of technology. Companies that did this well were certain to emerge as the world's most successful enterprises. This new era has served a very important role in helping all business leaders think more strategically about technology. But at the same time, the era of personal computers and connectedness have done little to help build understanding of why big, complex systems and IT projects take so long and cost so much. And that's where the rub is. What we do in software and technology is abstract and difficult to understand.

It's easy to visualize a new stadium. We get to see the architect's renderings and watch the building take shape. We can track the cost and schedule in very tangible ways. Technology projects are much different. Even though it costs just as much and takes just as long, building an application with two of million lines of code is a very foreign concept to most people. There is very little to look at along the way and great opportunity for misunderstanding.

I have found that the more dialogue that occurred between business leaders and technology leaders, the better the outcome. In fact, I believe to this day that the number one critical success factor for delivering IT solutions that meet expectations is relationship. When the relationship between the business and technology is strong, the project tends to succeed. When the relationship is

7

weak, the project will struggle and often fails. Let's face it, our science is still very new. The notion of exacting blue prints and engineering specifications that remove ambiguity are simply not there yet. So, it is incumbent on us, the business technology leaders of today's modern enterprises, to communicate in ways that bridge the gap.

Ashwin Rangan has lived the CIO role and observed the nuances of success and struggles. In Tomorrow's CIO, he puts forth much sound advice around how to navigate this complex and continuously changing space. Being an Insightful CIO seems to be a difficult calling, but in the end, it all boils down to insightful leadership through hard work, technical acumen, strong communication skills, strong relationships and earned trust. So next time you have the opportunity to chat with your CEO or your board of directors, don't tell them about the machine or the network. Tell them about the business possibilities you see. Or better yet, tell them about your kid's baseball game this weekend.

Rob Carter

Robert B. Carter, is Executive Vice President, FedEx Information Services and Chief Information Officer at FedEx Corporation, a $33b company that provides the transportation industry's broadest range of services.

Tomorrow's CIO is the first of a series published by the **Insightful CIO Group,** an IT-business consulting firm providing print, web, and interactive tools for the IT leaders of tomorrow. Please feel welcome to visit www.insightfulcio.com for updates, news, and other helpful tools.

Content

"You don't write because you want to say something, you write because you have something to say."

F. Scott Fitzgerald

Why Strategic Conversations?

There are many books written about Information Technology every year, most of them about specific technologies that help specific audiences with specific needs. Only some are about leveraging these technologies for the benefit of organizations, and very few discuss the people dynamics behind the leveraging and managing these technologies.

This book is for people who have chosen to leverage and manage Information Technology at the senior-most level of their profession. It is specifically written for the current and future Heads of IT in organizations, loosely referred to in the book as the CIO, regardless of specific organizational title.

Secondly, this book is for the executives who are chartered create optimal leverage from their IT investments and extract maximum value. These include CEOs, CFOs, and COOs.

Finally, aligning IT with the Board is a recurring topic in discussions at company headquarters. Directors and Advisors serving on the board of organizations will find useful and easy-to-apply frameworks in this book.

"Tomorrow's CIO: Strategic Executive Conversations " is the first of three books. These strategic conversations are those that occur between the CIO, the organization's Board, the CEO, the CFO and the COO. These are discussions wherein the participants are most likely to be focused on strategy most of the time; and the alignment of those strategies with intended IT investments and activities.

The intended outcome of the first book is to enable the reader to go away with perspectives and tools that help him gain a good and compelling understanding of the strategic aspirations of the organization and its ground realities.

What Next?

There will be a second book titled "Alignment Conversations." Using some of the frameworks and constructs that are developed in the first book, the second book explores conversations between the CIO and the other "CxO"s in the organization-the Chief Marketing Officer (CMO), the Head of Supply Chain Management, the Head of Sales, and so on. The outcome of the second book is intended to equip the reader with a process by which he can align the thoughts of his colleagues with the over-arching strategic aspirations of the organization, while keeping in sight the ground-realities of the organization.

The third book in the series, "Implementation Conversations," will explore the means through which a CIO translates the organization's strategic aspirations into execution tactics and techniques, leveraging the IT organization and its capabilities. The intended outcome of the third book is to arm the reader with a set of prescriptive steps that lead to realizing strategic alignment of IT within an organization—equipping and enabling the reader to make the proverbial rubber meet the road.

Ideas that influenced this book

In my experience, I have found books on topics such as this take one of three forms. The first form is where the author has engaged in primary research. After collecting, collating and processing data directly from the source, the author distils and extracts the essence of research. These results are then presented to the intended audience in a structured format, highlighting the essence. Usually, this exercise is both laborious and time-consuming; and typically, it leads to some deep insight that is not evident in just surface-scanning the area of interest.

The second form is where the author has directly interviewed authentic sources of information in the chosen field. Through this process, he discovers repeating patterns. Such patterns then get labeled as "best-practices." These are then presented to the intended audience as panaceas, to be "deployed-as-is-for-predictable-results."

This is a book of the third form: that of derivatives. It is built around concepts and approaches that I have gleaned from books that I have read over the decades, and from my own experiences. At its foundation is the distillate of four books and frameworks developed by other authors. I have leveraged this excellent foundation to build a superstructure with my experience, thoughts, and ideas. While none of the other books directly addressed the topic of being a Chief Information Officer, their work helped me frame my thoughts—and thereby, my behaviors and operating characteristics—over the years.

Early Questions, Few Answers

I risk dating myself here, but this was in the mid-1980s. I was a freshly minted graduate, just entering the systems field. I had lots of questions about what I was doing, and what I should be doing... "Should I be concerned with business processes? Or technologies? Or products?" It was rather bewildering that I did not know which processes were important than the others, and my world-view was limited to projects that I was assigned by my supervisor. And trade magazines were severely limited about technology at that time.

I was also somewhat awed by how the head of IT so suavely communicated technology in layman terms to his peers and superiors, in the first company I worked. These were areas of both interest and intrigue to me. I was thirsty for knowledge that would enable me to fill these gaps. I began to focus on technologies, rather than on the application of technologies, and only later—after some early disappointments and introspection—did I become more careful about what worked for the business. I then started to look for books and people to help me fill the gaps. And so began a wonderful journey of discovery.

The four books that shaped my thoughts to create the foundation for this book are *Reengineering the Corporation, The Discipline of Market Leaders, Leveraging the New Infrastructure, and Living on the Fault Line*. In this, I must thank my mostly-absent tutors.

Unrelated to this book, I have had the pleasure of interacting with some of them over the years, and without exception, they are brilliant thinkers and powerful projectors of big ideas. In the early 1990s, reading *Reengineering the Corporation* by Michael Hammer and James Champy had a profound impact on me. At that time, I was managing IT at AST Computer, a PC-manufacturer in Southern California. The then-CIO, Chet Lakhani, introduced me to it. Reading *Reengineering the Corporation* was like reading a book of self-evident "truths." I shared the book with several colleagues, who all concurred that the book was a great read. We agreed that the book could serve as a path-finder to break-through simplification of processes. AST at the time went through a transition of CIOs, and Richard Diamond came in as CIO. He was already a student of the book, and soon enough, his responsibilities expanded to include Business Process Reengineering (BPR) as a formal addition to the IT portfolio. It was then that I started to play a lead role in the BPR initiatives at AST Computer. My personal epiphany was that processes trumped technology in value enhancement for a business.

A couple of years later, Diamond introduced me to the next book that started to refine my process thinking. It was *The Discipline of Market Leaders*, by Michael Treacy and Fred Wiersema. In their book, Treacy and Wiersema created a framework that categorized businesses into three specific "value disciplines." They characterized a value discipline as an activity that is obsessively at the forefront of thinking in both the individual and collective minds of the senior team—essentially, the senior team mindset that creates and fosters the culture of the business. They hypothesized that over time, this becomes the bedrock of the business, its DNA.

Treacy and Wiersema characterized businesses as (1) Product Leadership businesses; (2) Operational Excellence businesses; and (3) Customer Intimate businesses. The clarity with which the authors explained these three value disciplines was exciting to me. It led me to question AST's own value discipline, and when the answer was not easily forth-coming in conversations with senior executives, it became clear—for the very first time again to me—why the CIO function struggles so mightily to find strategic alignment in many organizations!

A couple of years later, I moved on to Rockwell International's Semiconductor Division to head Business Process Reengineering. Soon, the IT function was tagged on to my responsibilities. I found this to be an ideal combination, wherein, as the leader of this combined portfolio, my team and I could shape the business processes first; and then apply appropriate technology solutions to reduce friction in the conduct of the process. And yet, our team struggled to find a clear framework to explain our activities. We were still doing a lot outside of the articulated value discipline axis of the business.

In the course of these years, Rockwell invited Dr. Michael Hammer for a private session with the CEOs of all business units and the incumbent business-unit CIOs. Dr Hammer's messages and manner of delivery were both forceful and clear. His fast-paced but deeply insightful session explained a lot. Yet, a few of my questions as a practicing CIO lingered.

Half-way there, yet...

I now knew how to integrate business process re-engineering with IT. I also knew how to probe the business for its unique value discipline. However, I could not (yet!) characterize IT spending in a coherent framework. I was still searching for a compelling framework that could enable me to differentiate IT investments in a manner that is easily communicated and as easily understood.

Later that year, we invited Dr. Michael Treacy to address the senior team for all of Rockwell International. Like Dr Hammer, Dr Treacy is a terrific orator: brilliant, forceful and convincing in his arguments. His message was to define, develop and make accretive investments along the chosen value-discipline axis to create sustainable business value. This supported his perspective, no doubt, but I still sought answers.

1998. The internet boom was in full swing. And I discovered *Leveraging the New Infrastructure* by Peter Weill and Marianne Broadbent. And in doing so, I learned the framework that clearly articulated how IT investments could be characterized in a 4-pane framework. A light-bulb went on! Most of the unanswered questions in my head started to get resolved. But...there were still a few last questions that remained unanswered.

Two more years went by. We had spun out the Semiconductor Division as an independent business: Conexant Systems Inc., and went on to list it on the NASDAQ. Conexant was newly-independent, in the middle of a transformation in the semiconductor chip sector, and struggling to find its value discipline. In a rapidly-commoditizing business environment, we felt that its value discipline should be Customer Intimacy (more later). And so we invited Fred Wiersema to tell us more. Wiersema did a lot to better explain how and why Customer Intimacy businesses succeed. And yet the CIO in me still struggled to piece together the last few pieces of the jigsaw puzzle.

2000. That euphoric year when the world was talking IT-speak, what with Y2K, ERP, the Internet and so on. I happened to get a copy of a new book by Geoffrey Moore called *Living on the Fault Line.*

In that wonderful book, Moore introduced the concept of Core versus Context. I read it and the final jigsaw puzzle pieces suddenly fell into place (I had to wait another 7 years before having an opportunity—no, the privilege—of meeting with Geoff Moore!) So this book is not an original work based on research and analysis. Nor is it a book based on interviews with subject matter experts. It is instead a synthesis of ideas gleaned, principally, from these four books. It is an exposition of the synthesis of these powerful ideas in my head. It led me from relative darkness to brilliant clarity.

I have successfully leveraged these learnings in the last few years to lead a few IT organizations, both large and small. In reading this book, I hope that your journey is shorter than mine, but that the destination is just as clear and brilliant.

Ashwin Rangan

Two clarifications

It is difficult to write a book without the use of personal pronouns. At the same time, it is unwieldy to use the "he or she" construct, and the "s/he" construct tends to look a bit artificial. I have therefore chosen to use a generic "he" or "she" interchangeably throughout the book. This is by no means a gender attribution. It is merely a way to focus on the message rather than on the gender of the actor in question. The reader will also see the words "Organization", "Business", "Enterprise" and "Company" throughout the book. I have chosen to use these words interchangeably. Once again, I feel that these words are somewhat inexactly equivalent.

Ashwin Rangan

Reading and after

I have provided a set of summarizing inferences, and questions to provoke the reader's thinking. If you would wish to continue with this thinking and initiate a dialogue, please feel welcome to visit the website, insightfulcio.com where we will be hosting a series of forums, discussions, and debates with peers, CIOs, and other C-level executives.

Ashwin Rangan
arangan@insightfulcio.com

Advance praise

"No one is more qualified to write THE BOOK about CIO success. Ashwin redefines executive excellence and extends the performance parameters of technology leadership. His experience in large and small enterprises, in giant organizations and start-ups operating in multiple vertical markets gives him a unique perspective on IT leadership. Read this book and improve your future."

Thornton May
Currently: Futurist & Dean, IT Leadership Academy

"One of the most critical success factors for a CIO is not just the ability to communicate with other C-level executives, but how to truly engage. Ashwin's eloquence and insight makes this a highly relevant and timely book. I could not only relate to his perspective, but found some techniques that I had not thought of and will put to use. It has the perfect blend of common sense and survival techniques for razor-edge political conditions."

Barbra Cooper
Currently: Group Vice President and CIO,
Toyota Motor Sales USA Inc.

"I thought [your book] was very well written. You made a number of points that I found myself nodding in agreement. Using "Core" for the IT systems and services that enable the business beyond ... is a provocative use of the word. Changes the focus of what IT should be doing. "

Norm Fjeldheim

Current - Senior Vice President and CIO, Qualcomm Inc.

"Your book is interesting, easy to read, very understandable, specific enough to provide value but general enough to apply to many. It is truly insightful."

Cheryl Smith

Former EVP and CIO, McKesson Corporation
Currently CEO, Utility.net

"This is an excellent book for any current or future CIO to read and think about."

David Phillips

Former EVP and CIO, Fluor Daniels Inc.
Currently Founding Partner, Peer Consulting

"The most successful companies in the world leverage technology to achieve a competitive advantage. There

Ashwin Rangan

is no way to reach this goal without alignment of CEO and CIO strategies. Ashwin Rangan's book Strategic Conversations delivers practical insights to help companies achieve this hard-to-find alignment and begin the journey to IT-powered success."

MR Rangaswami
Former Global Vice President (Marketing), Baan Software, Oracle Corporation and Avalon Software Co-Founder & Managing Director, Sand Hill Group

"The book is fantastic! It's [a] business book...that I did not want to put down. It's the kind of book that I searched for back when I was starting out and could not find. It would go absolutely perfectly with an MBA course, or for anyone wanting to understand the interplay between IT and their organization. You have a winner!"

Rich Hoffman
President, Hyundai Information Services North America (HISNA)

"Your writing reflects the wisdom you have gathered over the years in highly responsible positions. "

Gene Goda

Former Chairman, Simulation Sciences Inc.,
Meridian Software Systems Inc. and ObjectShare Inc.
Currently Board Member, Powerwave Technologies Inc.

"I have read your book and love it. It is excellent! "

Jerre MJ Stead

Former Chairman and CEO, Ingram Micro, Legent,
AT&T Inc. Currently Chairman and CEO, IHS

"Ashwin's book brings uncommon "common" sense to all that interact with the CIO function; a must read for all CxOs."

Andy King

Currently Head of IT, SitOnIt

"Rangan has written an east-to-read but very thoughtful book. While a short read, the list of actions for myself that came out of reading this book leaves me plenty to consider, plan, or act on; and I'll finish a better CIO."

Jeffrey Reid

Currently Head of IT, Totota Material Handling Systems

Ashwin Rangan

"I found your book interesting, written in a "matter of fact" manner, easy to relate to and most importantly.... I loved the quotations and the personal stories. Great job on writing such an insightful book!"

Bala Govender
Currently VP of IT, Jazz Semiconductors

"I must commend you for the style and the language: simple yet effective, easy-flowing yet well-connected to other parts, general to draw parallels but specific and actionable for those who want to develop additional insight. It is rare to see the combination of these traits rolled into one. "

Ram Mynampati
President, Satyam Technologies Inc.

"A very useful book for the CIO community. Today's CIOs should have the weight to carry themselves in the C-suite...and this book arms them with the needed skills."

Don Beall
Former Chairman and CEO, Rockwell International Inc.
Former Board Member, Proctor & Gamble Inc.

"I like the way it is written and thought the contents were great."

Jim Sutter

Former CIO, Rockwell International Inc.

Currently Partner, Peer Consulting

"Today, IT is like oxygen.... like the air we breathe. It is everywhere. In writing this book, you are on to something here!"

Edward Merino

Former Chairman, Forum for Corporate Directors

Currently CEO and Founder, Office of the Chairman

Section 1: Seeking Strategy

"Technology is just a tool. In terms of getting the kids working together and motivating them, the teacher is the most important."

Bill Gates,
Chairman of the Board, Microsoft

What does the CIO stand for in an organization? The Chief Information Officer? Or the Chief Irrelevant Officer? First, the person with the title has the opportunity to define it. It is only later that others are able to judge whether the person is the former or the latter.

Chief Executive Officers (CEOs) struggle with defining the full scope of the roles and responsibilities of their CIOs, even as businesses struggle with evaluating the return-on-investment (ROI) from their Information Technology investments. The value of IT continues to be a hotly-debated —perhaps especially, in CIO circles—and interestingly enough, it has raged on for over 20 years, about roughly the same time that I have been associated with the IT profession. Various CIO magazines regularly talks about a revolving-door that turns a full circle, in anywhere from 24 to 48 months. Macabre jokes abound, citing CIOs who don't unpack boxes when they get to a new desk at a new job—just so that their next move is easy and quick. Jokes aside, this is an issue that demands to be better understood. If indeed there is a problem, we should better understand that problem so that we—as a profession—can take steps to resolve it.

Chapters 1 through 4 in this book address the position and role of a CIO, the attributes that a CEO should seek in his CIO, and the thoughtful and strategic alignment of the CIO function within an organization. Finding and slotting an effective CIO is critical for a CEO, especially if IT-enablement is an integral element of value-delivery in the business. Which business today

Ashwin Rangan

does not have IT-enablement as a vital element in its value-creation or value-delivery chain?

So getting the "right" CIO is first and foremost about a CEO's thoughtful introspection of his enterprise. Only later is it about the effectiveness and efficiency of the individual who chooses to serve as a CIO.

This section is about the CEO and CIO of a business explicitly co-discovering and stating the strategy of the business, structurally aligning the CIO function for success, and creating the right business and cultural environment to support the CIO's initiatives and efforts for optimal business benefits.

1. Pomp and Circumstance Of The CIO

"The secret of all victory lies in the organization of the non-obvious."

Marcus Aurelius

I t is important to set the tone for this book in the context of an organization. Organization structures are of many forms, depending on whether the organization is for-profit or not, the primary value proposition of the organization and the view point of the CEO and the Board. In other words, there is no 'one shape fit all' in organization design.

Organizations grow and shrink over time. As they do so, it has become necessary to codify the business

Ashwin Rangan

processes that make them function on a day to day basis. Since the earliest days of business, such processes have been recorded. With the advent of computers and networked information systems, business process records have become increasingly automated and computerized. The art and the emerging science of orchestrating this is the role that is typically fulfilled by the Chief Information Officer, or the CIO.

An important note here: Not all organizations call their head of Information technology the CIO. Some call them CIO, while others label the position the Vice President of IT. Still others refer to them as the Director of IT. In some cases, I have seen the label of Head of IT. The point here is that the specific label is relatively unimportant. What is important is the nature and relevance of the role in the context of the organization structure.

Is there a "typical" organization structure?

I am sure you have heard of the "typical family." In this "typical family," there are "typically" 4.23 people in the family, with "typically" 0.63 pets and an average annual income of $45,349! (Hate to be that .23 fraction in that typical family!) In other words, these are statistical abstractions of an underlying reality that varies from one family to the next. Likewise, it is impossible to "typify" an organization structure; however, we will use the following organization structure to provide a context to this book. It is reflective of a large, product-centric, multi-national organization.

Your own organization may be exactly—or somewhat closely resembling—this structure, or could be very dissimilar to it. The key is to understand the background against which you serve as the head of IT. When you remove this contextual understanding, it becomes difficult to ground your activities appropriately.

The scope and scale of your initiatives are often dictated by the specific position that you enjoy in

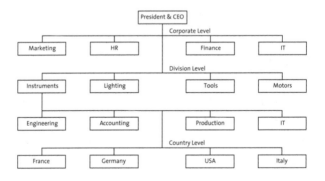

the overall organizational context. In our example organization, there are three distinct levels at which a CIO may function.

- one where the CIO is at the very top, at the so-called "Corporate" level
- one could be where the CIO at the next level down. This is typically the "Divisional" level.
- or one could be a CIO at the next level down at the "Country" level.

It is very important here to pause and explore some nuances and their connotations.

In exiting the first paragraph, I referred to this organization as "reflective of a large, product-centric, multi-national organization." The sequence of phrases is an important nuance.

In this example, product-centricity trumps multi-nationality. In such an organization, country operations are likely to be offshoots from product-centric structures at the center. Each country's structure is therefore likely to be a reflection—more likely smaller—of the structure at the center.

Very often, such an organization has a CIO at the corporate level. For example, when I served as CIO at Rockwell International, there was a Corporate CIO, and I was one of a group of Divisional CIOs serving various divisions of Rockwell like Rockwell Automotive, Rockwell Collins, Rockwell Automation, Rockwell Electronic Commerce and, in my case, Rockwell Semiconductors. Many, if not all, of these divisions had a country-presence, ranging from just a few to several thousands, in several countries around the world.

If an organization's country operations are large enough, a CIO function may be warranted for each operating division in every country-like the CIO for Toyota Financial Services in the US, for example. If the relative size of the operation does not warrant it, there may just be a Country CIO for the overarching brand in the country. When I served in the CIO organization at Wal-Mart, for instance, there was a country CIO in the Mexico. Wal-Mart operated under multiple store-banners in Mexico.

In some very large organizations, the structure is reflective of a large, multi-national, product-centric organization. Again, the sequence of phrases is note-

Ashwin Rangan

worthy. In such an organization, there are 3 levels, just as in the previous example. However, following the corporate level the next level in the hierarchy is the country, followed by the brands that are specific to that country. Such an organization tends to be a loosely-coupled federation of country-centric operations, where the business is governed at the country level and the brands are managed within the context of the country.

There is no "right" structure for an organization, although there are many wrong ones. A few accepted norms have emerged over time that organizations have experimented with and adopted.

Finally, it is also worth noting that structures have oscillated between centralization and decentralization, with all the attendant hyperbole and problems. With computing, storage, communications, and networking capabilities becoming both ubiquitous and increasingly affordable, some of the concepts that historically led to decentralization have come under greater scrutiny. Since these new technology capabilities have enabled businesses to "shrink time and distance," it has led some of the largest brands in the world—like Cisco, for instance—to organize their IT environment as large, centralized, product-centric, multi-national organizations.

Framework for your thoughts

Like the canvas and framework to a painting, the organizational structure chart is not the end-product, but serves to provide the end-product with a background and boundaries. As a CIO serving at any level in the organization, this context gives you a basic framework to determine how much autonomy you have on the job. It gives you a framework to question and clarify what is negotiable and, more important, what is not negotiable.

For instance, the corporate CIO at Rockwell International provided wide-area networking infrastructure for all businesses—a facility that emerged as a requirement from all the divisions in the business. Leveraging the strength of the brand and the aggregated demand volume, the CIO and his team negotiated with vendors to drive down the cost-per-unit of networking infrastructure and services, while always bearing in mind the quality of service required to support the various business unit' unique needs. This was then presented as a corporate utility to the divisions. Ordinarily, no single division would have been able to get a utility service at such a comparable rate because it would lack the negotiating leverage of the combined group. As a Division CIO, while I was not mandated to use the wide-area networking services provisioned by the Corporate CIO, fiscal prudence demanded that I justify every deviation request.

Summary

Organizations have a formal chart that depicts the business functions as a series of interrelated blocks of activity. It is important to understand the structural linkages and implicit hierarchies in such a chart. These are significant data points in determining the scope, size, autonomy and control implicit in your role as a CIO.

Good CIOs function well when the organization structure and context is described clearly to them.

Great CIOs take this context as the starting point and then dive deeper into the usually less well-developed interfaces—between country and division, or between division and corporate. They detect how these interfaces may be hindering the day-to-day flows of information.

The Insightful CIO—at all levels, be it country, division or corporate—shares in the vision of the enterprise. He helps the enterprise to leverage technologies that enable the easy flow of information enterprise-wide, regardless of the artificial boundaries that typically define organization structures. He implicitly understands that organization structures are meant to clarify control structures, not ossify them.

Insights and probes

1. Organizations can be both large and complex. Sometimes, size dictates complexity. And sometimes, age of the organization and generational evolution breeds complexity. It takes vigilance and relentless effort to keep IT simple amidst change and growth. How would you characterize your organization? Large? Complex? Both?

2. Organizations can be global or multi-national.

Global organizations tend to have strong centers, with policies and practices centrally defined, but administered in a decentralized fashion. Multi-national organizations, on the other hand, tend to have many different centers. From a financial perspective, they typically have a strong center at the notional corporate headquarters. From an operational perspective, they typically have strong national centers. How is your enterprise organized?

3. The context of operations for IT is often defined by the structural location of the CIO functions in the enterprise hierarchy. Can you picture and draw the exact structural location(s) of IT in your enterprise hierarchy?

Mental modeling for the neophyte

1. Organization design is one of the abstractions that enable an enterprise to function at all. If you had a clean slate, would you design the structure of your enterprise as it currently stands? What would you alter? How? Why?

2. Global brands typically have large and complex organization structures. Do you work in one such? Or know a professional colleague in such an enterprise? Have you discussed organization structure and the position of IT in that context with him?

3. Think of a very large and global brand. Say Procter and Gamble. Now, imagine that you are the newly-appointed CIO of P&G. How would you theorize your going-in position? What would you expect to find? Do you have any notions about how the IT function in P&G ought to be structured? Discuss this with a trusted colleague or a mentor.

2. The Six Juggling Acts of a CIO

"The trick to juggling is determining which balls are made of rubber and which ones are made of glass."

Anonymous

The Insightful CIO is a consummate juggler, gracefully managing the multiple demands of both business and technology. He is the bridge between the world of business and the world of IT. As the bridge connecting two banks, he has to be well-rooted both on the bank that caters technology to the business and on the bank that leverages technology for the benefit of the business. The CIO discerns those technologies that best fit the needs of the organization at any given time. He then moves the organization to embrace the flow of those technologies enthusiastically, thereby realizing value. Extending the metaphor, it is interesting to note that the river of technologies continues to move faster between these two banks.

You can see that there is a dichotomy here—between "the business" and "IT." This dichotomy is quite real, even though IT has been around for over half a century. Ask any CIO who has been in the saddle for more than a year—he will relate to this statement very well.

Good CIOs are interpreters and communicators of messages that are crafted differently by these two different worlds. Great CIOs syndicate, authenticate and "conduct" messages across these two worlds, just as music conductors engender enthralling music from a diverse and delicate Philharmonic Orchestra.

The Insightful CIOs make this difficult—and sometimes impossible—job look easy and effortless! Try juggling with just two tennis balls, and you will know.

Characterizing the business world

The world of business is dynamic, ever-fascinating, and needless to say, highly complex. At the core of well-run businesses is a set of business processes—naturally linked activities that take a set of disparate inputs and transform them to one or more outputs that are valuable to the paying customer. Almost all businesses have a fairly similar set of business processes: new product development process, go-to-market process, order-to-cash process, supply-chain process, requisition-to-check process, customer acquisition and retention process etc.

While this catalog and taxonomy of processes is similar—if not identical—within (certainly) the same business segment, the emphasis on certain sets of processes varies from business to business. This is how businesses choose to put distance between themselves and the competition.

Over the years, every business discovers the specific set of processes that command a premium from its customers. In well-defined industry verticals, it is rare for a business to articulate a chosen set of processes first, and then commence doing business with its customers along those processes. A challenger—like a JetBlue in the airlines industry, or a Barefoot Winery in the wines industry—sometimes emerges suddenly. In fact, such challengers attack the incumbents with a new set of strategies and processes that defy the hitherto "conventional wisdom."

Once these processes gain traction within the organization, they become ingrained. They are accepted as the core competency in that business. A certain discipline sets in to safe-guard and to govern them. The organization's DNA starts to gel and set. Businesses typically become expert at repeatedly re-discovering this discipline. The best of businesses are usually harshest in judging their own competence in this area. Great businesses go from being obsessively compulsive in delivering value through this competency to selecting leaders who have an intuitive grasp of and a flair for furthering this discipline.

In their wonderful book The Discipline of Market Leaders, Treacy and Wiersema called this the "value discipline." According to them, the value discipline of any given business can usually be categorized into one of three kinds:

1 A business that demonstrates product leadership;
2 A business built on operations excellence; or
3 A business that has built customer intimacy.

In the course of my career, I have had the great good fortune to work in businesses that exhibited and excelled at these three different value disciplines. Where applicable, I will draw from my experience and illustrate my points with personal examples.

Good CIOs try to address business needs based on the dictates of their business partners. Insightful CIOs work with their C-level colleagues to extract the essence of the nature of the business—the core competency of the business—and crystallize it as the value discipline for the benefit of the entire team. And over time, they and their teams add value to that one competitive dimension of the business that categorizes the business most appropriately. In this process, they help their chosen business achieve distinction.

Juggling balls in the Information Technology world
The world of IT is also quite complex, and this said,
IT can be resolved as being a combination of six
fundamental activities:

1. Infrastructure provisioning: Typically hardware
   oriented; concerned with connectivity, computing,
   storage, feeds and speeds;

2. Applications management: Typically software
   oriented related to Engineering, Business
   management and so on;

3. Operations management: Ensuring hardware and
   software are appropriately available where and
   when needed;

4. Quality Assurance and on-time release
   management: Making sure that deployed
   hardware and software actually do what they are
   advertised to do;

5. Project and Program management: An increasingly
   more important aspect of IT, which deals with
   insuring that projects and programs adhere to a
   pre-disclosed "portfolio" that has been aligned to
   pre-established goals and measures—in terms of
   deliverables, cost and time; and

6 Risk Management, especially as IT is becoming increasingly intertwined in numerous aspects of business: As its ubiquity increases with time, IT-induced risks spread out. IT's intricacies are not always clearly explained or fully understood in many organizations, leading to unintended consequences.

Good CIOs conduct these six sets of activities well so that the businesses they help to lead receive the most from their IT investments. In collaboration with his C-suite colleagues, the Insightful CIO sets up a set of transparent mechanisms to invest in, and harvest benefits from, these six sets of activities.

Summary

The world-view of business professionals is considerably different from the world-view of IT professionals. Business people deal with the day-to-day reality of defining, developing and delivering customer value. IT professionals deal with abstracting these into symbolic forms and re-representing them in machine-language for the benefit of the business. Good CIOs understand that there are two different worlds. They choose to operate on "their side of the fence," building good IT assets that can be leveraged by the business. Insightful CIOs create a bridge between these two different worlds. They use this bridge frequently, so that the line that divides business from IT increasingly blurs over time. Building and using such a bridge, CIOs not only create greater value based on deeper understanding of mutual leverage, but also create mutual trust that they can continually enrich and exercise.

Insights and probes

1. The CIO is a Chief, a leader of people. His special charter is to provide appropriate information technology solutions to serve the business that he co-leads. Are you regarded as a Chief in your business? If not, why not?

2. The primary objective of the CIO is to help elucidate the nature of the business and then, serve the needs of that business with the right set of computer and related information technologies.

What is the nature of your business?

3. The secondary objective of the CIO is to plan, organize, staff, manage and control a team of IT professionals. This team's charter is to provision and manage information technologies to support the business. How much time would you say has been devoted to planning and organizing the IT function in your business? Do you feel you have the right people in the right spots? Or is there room for substantial improvement? If so, what is keeping you from making these changes?

4. A natural by-product of this set of activities should be to measure and report progress against goals in all six core-competency areas. What sort of report-outs do you have in your IT organization? Who defined them? Who reviews them? How frequently? Do you get feedback from the business? What happens after you receive feedback?

Mental modeling for the neophyte

1. Do you understand the primary competitive axis of your business? Request your CIO to make this a discussion item when next you have a one-on-one conversation with him.

2. Assess your own capabilities in the six core-competencies required of the CIO function. Do you have a working understanding of each of these six areas? If not, what avenues are available to you to develop these competencies?

Ashwin Rangan

3. The Nine Unique Attributes of the Insightful CIO

"The best executive is the one who has sense enough to pick good men to do what he wants done, and self-restraint to keep from meddling with them while they do it."

Theodore Roosevelt

The role of the CIO has undergone tremendous evolution in a relatively short period of time, when measured in business terms. After all, in the broadest of senses, business has been transacted ever since the first two creatures bartered goods. It is easy to look back and see that information technology—the under-pinning need that mandates a CIO function in a business—has undergone tremendous evolution in the last 30-50 years. As IT capabilities have evolved, so has the role of the head of that aspect of business. Given this context, it is now easier to understand why the attributes of the person responsible for this functional area in the business has had to change. It is also easy to understand why CIOs who were regarded in awe as recently as a decade ago, may be experiencing difficulty in coping.

By definition, good CIOs are experts in the domain knowledge of information technology. Technologies change quickly, requiring the CIO as an individual to be someone who can change and adapt as quickly, if not more quickly. Great CIOs are 360-degree individuals. They sense and internalize the changing role that their own function entails, all the while being aware of changes occurring in the technology domain; and yet concurrently being a vigilant partner to the business that they serve.

In essence, great CIOs are rare professionals. They are ever alert, aware and vigilant.

The Insightful CIO - How exactly is he different?

At the highest level, the CIO is alert to changes in the IT space, aware of changes in the business that he serves, and vigilant in ensuring that IT's relevance to the business is never compromised.

Given the role of the CIO and the nature of this individual's contributions, the question that is often asked is, "Should the CIO be a business person with IT knowledge, or a technical person with business understanding?" The answer to this question has changed over time.

In the early 1970s, the answer might have been, "A technical person with business understanding." In those early days of computing, when the focus was on technology, it was relatively a novelty in businesses, poorly understood by the vast majority, and too expensive for all but large enterprises. Today, the pendulum has swung to where an increasingly larger number of companies will likely answer, "A business person with IT knowledge." So what is the difference between these two kinds of people?

The difference is their world-view: a business person

is comfortable dealing with shades of grey, while a technical person will force-fit the world into zones of black and white.

Business people tend to be comfortable with rough generalities—concepts and ideas move such a person. Technical people tend to be more comfortable with details—concepts and ideas are great; but how do we get them implemented? A businessman focuses on the "why" and the "what," whereas a technical person quickly starts to worry about the "how," "who," and "when." Today's great CIOs tend to be excellent at dealing with shades of grey and complexity. This apart, I have observed some common traits amongst my peers who have excelled. They all seemed to share in a subset of nine unique attributes. The awesome ones have mastered all nine.

The nine unique attributes of the Insightful CIO

The Insightful CIO is a Visionary. He has the ability to envision dreams that bridge the needs of the business with the capabilities of technology, either now or quickly accessible just over the horizon.

Ashwin Rangan

The Insightful CIO is a Communicator. He can paint his dreams on the canvas of his audiences' minds, with brushes made of powerful words. His talk is in easily-understood, non-technical terms for the business community; and simultaneously, in easily-understood business terms for the IT community. He is a story-teller who can get people excited to commit to a journey that will lead the collective to a "better" place.

The Insightful CIO is a Strategist. He has the ability to balance a variety of dynamic business and technical variables, while bearing the end-goal always and clearly in mind. The CIO is open to new information and ideas; and has the strength of character to change course and commitments if warranted by changing circumstances, while manifesting the fortitude to commit resources all along the way.

The Insightful CIO is a Change-agent. He assists the leadership team to discover the most pressing changes that the business has to undertake. As both the steward of sources of information and the creator of conduits for information, the CIO has a unique vantage point. Given a change initiative, he knows the various aspects of the business that will be touched by the proposed change. The CIO is one of the few executives on the leadership team who is continually undertaking change initiatives. By virtue of this capability, the CIO develops a perspective on how to successfully chart a course to change. The Insightful CIO is the business' chosen partner, when it comes to change initiatives.

The Insightful CIO is a Director. He thinks like a mountain-climber. The CIO knows that every step involves the expenditure of scarce resources, and tries to make sure that each step is upwards, and edges the organization closer to the goal at the pinnacle of the mountain. If the current situation prevents this progression onward and upward, the CIO directs the activity to take a step sideways, so that ground is never lost in the process.

The Insightful CIO is a Planner. He is careful in committing resources. The CIO is constantly balancing three balls in the air while planning—Scope, Time and Money. He knows that money can be translated into resources, but that money cannot buy time or change the scope of activity.

The Insightful CIO is a Thinker. The CIO's domain is the commissioning and management of inanimate assets, where people breathe life into activities that, in turn, breathe life into these assets. Asset performance is a proxy for people performance in the CIO domain. He is constantly aware of the inter-play between people on the CIO team.

The Insightful CIO is a Doer. He has a bias for action. Technologies move and morph even while business needs are changing constantly. As a result, the zone of interaction between these two—the CIO's domain—changes rapidly. As changes in the two feeder environments occur only faster everyday, the CIO has to address acceleration as a central element of his "reality."

The Insightful CIO is a Human. He surrounds himself with competent, trust-worthy and reliable professionals. Colleagues share his passion, understand his vision and help him lead the IT organization so that

IT really works for the business. The CIO becomes the ring-master. He is thoughtful, considerate, and compassionate. The CIO brings a sense of balance and humor to his interactions with his team. He maintains perspective—being an agent of change when things are calm; and a calming influence in chaos.

Summary

Business changes constantly. So does information technology. The trick is for CIOs to help the business make sense of these changes. Good CIOs help their business partners understand how technology is changing. Insightful CIOs internalize both business changes and technology changes. They help their business partners to take advantage of business opportunities while leveraging changing—and more capable—technologies.

Insights and probes

1. The CIO is a "360 degree" individual. How

would you assess your own level of awareness, alertness and vigilance?

2. The CIO has to be "right" for the business. If cost-controls and efficiencies are the primary needs of the day, the business may warrant a CIO who is dominantly technical, but appreciates the nuances of business. On the contrary, if revenue-enhancement and IT effectiveness are the primary needs of the day, the business may warrant a CIO who is first a business person and then, a student of IT. What kind of a business do you serve? How flexible are your skills? Are you comfortable waxing and waning, in sync with the business? How "right" do you feel?

3. The CIO's worldview should map to the needs of the business. Otherwise, both the CIO and the business run the risk of being out-of-kilter with one another, leading to painful lack of alignment. The business will suffer! Does your world-view match that of the business that you serve?

4. CIOs are leaders, just like their other CXO colleagues. Given a nudge and time to gain domain understanding, CIOs can be (and are

increasingly becoming) good COOs and CEOs. And vice-versa—where COOs and CFOs are becoming good CIOs. Does the thought of changing responsibility—to serve as COO or CEO—excite you? Or is that a frightening thought? Why? What do you plan to do about it?

Mental modeling for the neophyte

1. Understand your level of awareness. Are you "on the ball" all the time?

2. Introspect on your understanding of the business world. Can you read a Balance Sheet? An Income Statement? A Cash Flow statement? Do all the lines on these make sense to you? (More about this later in the book.)

3. Assess your own world-view. Are you comfortable with shades of grey, or are you better off when the blacks and whites are resolved? Do you agree with the French author Voltaire, that "Perfect is the enemy of good enough?"

4. Sense for yourself, with complete candor, if you are

already a leader. If your current title says "Manager," ask yourself, "Where are my leadership gaps?" Engage in a dialog with your boss and with HR in a feedback session about your leadership gaps. Seek means to close the gaps.

5. If you are not comfortable leading teams of people, don't! There's nothing worse than a reluctant leader.

4. Should The CIO Report To The CEO?

"Leadership is the art of getting someone else to do something you want done because he wants to do it."

Dwight D. Eisenhower
34th President of the United States of America

The CEO sets the tone at the top. His voice is the voice of strategy, regardless of the enterprise. This tone sets the cadence for the business and it is the responsibility of the senior leadership to internalize this tone. These leaders, in turn, must interpret it for the benefit of their team members in the context of their specific domains.

In today's business, the dialog between the CEO and

the CIO has assumed critical importance, where, if this link is weak, the value of the "IT-enabled value-chain," is compromised—no matter what else the CIO may do.

IT is increasingly both more integrated into the core business and more expensive. In fact, in most industries, IT is second only to buildings and plants in CapEx investments. And yet, it is not always clear that the returns on this significant investment are quantifiable and consistent. This dialog is therefore crucial, so that the CEO "gets IT."

Good CIOs get the job done. The Insightful CIO not only gets the job done; but does it with transparency and dignity. The Insightful CIO can only be transparent and dignified with the understanding and active partnership of a CEO who "gets IT."

What is the CEO's interest in a business?

Great CEOs are primarily interested in the long-term value created by their businesses, and only after that, about the current quarter's performance.

Leaders of business create long-term values by making accretive investments in core competencies and harvesting them judiciously. These core competencies— or the value disciplines so well-articulated by Treacy and Wiersema—may have nothing to do with the product or service being offered the customer. To recall, the value discipline of any given business can usually be categorized into one of three kinds:

1. A business that demonstrates product leadership;
2. An organization built on operations excellence; or
3. A business that has built customer intimacy.

For example, Dell's value discipline is operational excellence, although its business products and services are focused on high-tech. Another example is Land's End. The value discipline for this organization is clearly customer intimacy, while its business products are mid- to high-end apparel. Likewise, the thought of Apple products immediately conjures the idea of innovation and product leadership.

CEOs typically start by investing in one of the three value disciplines. Over time, CEOs deliberately and persistently invest in the same discipline, at the expense of the other two. In doing this, CEOs seek to explicitly differentiate their business from the competition. Implicitly therefore, CEOs choose to seek parity or settle for sub-par capabilities along the other two disciplines relative to competition.

Just one value discipline? Why not two? Or all three?

The last section may make it appear that organizations can only pursue one value-discipline, to the exclusion of the other two. This is not the case at all. Businesses usually choose one of these value disciplines as a vector of departure and differentiation, relative to the competition. Over time, if successful, they master the chosen discipline. However, no business can expect to survive, leave alone thrive, if they do not make investments in the other disciplines. Therefore, successful businesses choose to over-invest in one discipline—the one that they want as a differentiator—while still investing in the other two. Only, they invest just enough to seek and gain parity with respect to the competition.

Businesses that are recognized as leaders in their markets choose to set the bar in the discipline that they choose to master. They make a conscious choice to meet the bar in the other two axes, allowing the competition to set the bar.

Gaining mastery demands focus, effort, resources and time. Large organizations with defensible business fundamentals and high barriers to new entrants can (and do) choose to invest in more than one value-discipline. They tend to pull away from their competition even faster when they are successful in doing so. Notable examples include such leadership organizations as Proctor & Gamble, for instance. P&G demonstrates both product leadership and operational excellence.

Very few CEOs lead their teams and companies to master even two of these value disciplines, let alone all three. Most well-run companies, with good financials to show for it, tend to be extremely good at one of the value disciplines, out-distancing the competition. Even such companies rarely choose to invest in a second value-discipline. As with any well-run businesses, these are investment choices—with concomitant trade-offs. So businesses willfully choose a differentiator to make focused investments. Equally willfully, they carefully benchmark and choose to invest just enough along the other value-discipline axes to gain parity in the marketplace.

How does a CIO discover and develop an insight about the business that he serves? This is a good question and deserves an answer that you, the reader, and I will discover together now.

Discovering the nature of "our" business together

The Insightful CIO makes an effort to understand the business' value discipline early on, even though the directed activities of an organization may not be a reflection of its value discipline. Again, as an example, Southwest Airlines is in the B2C (or business to consumer) business—serving individuals like you and me. One might imagine that Southwest Airlines' value discipline is therefore Customer Intimacy. Wrong. The value discipline of Southwest Airlines is Operational Excellence. Wal-Mart is storied as an Operational Excellence business, and I saw that first-hand when I served there as a CIO.

Rockwell Semiconductor Systems (RSS) in the early 1990s was a vertically-integrated semiconductor business. In this, RSS was a business driven by operational excellence. After it's IPO as Conexant Systems Inc., it underwent a painful but necessary business transition—from being a vertically integrated "soup-to-nuts" semiconductor manufacturer to becoming a fabless semiconductor business, emphasizing engineering design. Conexant made a brave, but futile re-engineering attempt to differentiate itself by focusing on customer intimacy. However, the markets it served demanded, and ultimately rewarded, businesses that delivered to the third value-discipline—product leadership. As someone in a front-and-center seat in this from start through the transition, it was gut-wrenching for me to take people through the transition, but even more so to re-jigger the IT underpinnings.

In the mid 1980s, AST Computer served its customers using the Value Added Reseller (VAR) channel. One of the founders of AST was masterful in orchestrating AST's VAR channel strategy, and I had the privilege of witnessing the Customer Intimacy value discipline from this vantage point.

Watch that language

Businesses—like people—tend to use a set of words and phrases repeatedly to drive home their value discipline. By examining these descriptive attributes, a CIO can discover the lexicon of the business he is in. The alert CIO will sort the verbiage of his colleagues. In doing so, he will develop his own insights into the value discipline of the business he serves. If the leadership team of a business is unfamiliar with the value discipline framework, the CIO will be unlikely to get a direct answer to his questions about the value-discipline of the business. In such cases, the CIO will be well-served to initiate dialogs about the value proposition of the business, the core processes of the organization, the levers for improvement, and the major business improvement challenges. Words and phrases in response to these probing dialogs will likely serve as directional indicators from which the CIO can infer the nature of the business. The CIO should then validate his impressions with further discussions and dialog— particularly with the CEO, CFO and the COO.

People in the Product Leadership businesses tend to use words and phrases such as "best product" in describing what they bring to the markets that they serve. They focus on time-based go-to-market strategies. They discuss first-mover advantages and fast-follower strategies. They obsess about "TAM" or Total Addressable Market. They are paranoid about market-share. They will demand to be Number One or Two in the markets that they serve. They often "eat their young" or "cannibalize" their products in offering next-generation capabilities and products to their customers. Such companies are remarkably technology-focused. Their core processes focus on value creation through invention and innovation.

The executive team use phrases such as "patent portfolio," "product pipeline," "portfolio management," and "keep-or-kill processes" to characterize how new products are selected and developed. It is quite common to experience obsessive paranoia about intellectual property in such businesses. Businesses like BMW in automotives, Genentech in bio-technology, Apple in consumer electronics and Qualcomm in semiconductors are good examples of such businesses.

Ashwin Rangan

People in Operational Excellence businesses are focused on "Total Landed Costs" of products and services that they deliver to the marketplace. In such businesses, any variability in the supply-chain—either on the sourcing and procurement side or the delivery side—leads to additional cost. These businesses look for continuous improvement in their core processes to "suck out" unnecessary frills. "Lean" and "fat" are often used to describe good and bad practices, and "Six-sigma" is the official "manna from heaven." Such businesses file for process patents rather than for product patents. Think of Ford in the early days, when our ancestor could buy a basic A- or T-Model in any color as long as it was black. Dell in PCs and Wal-Mart in retailing exemplify such businesses today.

Executives in the Customer Intimacy businesses are all about understanding the total "pain-chain" from the customer's point of view. Their catalog of offerings extends to encompass their customer's value-chain, from sourcing to delivery. Such businesses do not limit themselves to just what they supply. Instead, they take a more expansive view of how their products and services fit into the overall problem that their customer is trying to resolve. They like to embed themselves in their customer's shoes, and "walk in their customers' moccasins." In doing so, they understand the customer's broader problem. These businesses use words and phrases like "customer acquisition and development cost," "solutions provisioning," and "services customization." They pride themselves on knowing their customers' business in great detail. In my experience, Rockwell Automation was a classic example of a business that competed on Customer Intimacy. The following table, excerpted from *The Discipline of Market Leaders,* captures the essence of these three paradigms.

	Operational Excellence	Product Leadership	Customer Intimacy
Value Proposition	Best total cost	Best product	Best total solution
Golden Rule	Variety kills efficiency	Cannibalize success with breakthroughs	Solve the client's broader problem
Core Processes	End-to-end product delivery Customer service cycle	Invention Commercialization	Client acquisition Solution development
Improvement Levers	Process redesign Continuous improvement	Product technology R&D cycle time	Problem expertise Service optimization
Major Improvement Challenges	Shift to new asset base	Jump to new technology	Total change in solution paradigm

Figure 4.1 - The implications of value disciplines

The CIO should be aware and alerted to the fact that building a sustainable advantage from a single value discipline is in itself an effort that takes many years.

Jim Collins explains this well in From Good to Great. He uses the analogy of turning a flywheel. Great organizations identify the one flywheel that they will favor over all others. Perhaps unconsciously at first, but very consciously as time goes by, they focus all their effort and energy on building momentum for this flywheel. Soon enough, the flywheel spins fast, and with each turn, much less energy is required to keep it spinning. Each additional push only adds to the angular velocity of the flywheel, generating even more momentum. If you imagine this flywheel to be the impulsion mechanism in the business, then the business will continually put more distance between itself and the laggards in its competitive space, at a marginal incremental expenditure.

While an easy concept to grasp, it is not so easy to translate into action and measurable results.

How does this information help the Insightful CIO?

Getting to possess this information is the first key for the CIO to strategically align herself with the business. Let us look at each of the three value disciplines; and understand the appropriate stance that the Insightful CIO should adopt.

In Product Leadership businesses, the emphasis is on developing new Intellectual Property (IP). It is about leveraging IP to define and develop products. It is about bringing them to market at the fastest possible rate without breaking the bank.

Such businesses typically exist in an ecosystem where product cycles are relatively short, and time-to-market is the key to maximize profits.

The Insightful CIO begins by understanding the new-product development process well, and becomes intimately familiar with the flow of information—the classical triad of inputs, processes and outputs—that accompanies the entire value-chain from product ideation through product launch. Then, she recognizes potential bottle-necks or "impedance points" in the process that could jam the information flow from thought to launch. Armed with these insights, she can align IT investments and efforts appropriately.

In such businesses, the CIO is well-advised to create a close working relationship with the business unit General Managers. These businesses typically tend to charter GMs with both Marketing and Product Development. The Insightful CIO becomes a trusted advisor to the GMs. Her role in this relationship is to continually bring IT solutions to the table that helps the GMs collect and collate Intellectual Property (IP); to sort through ideas that purport to monetize IP; to understand the economics of choosing to keep or kill products in the development pipeline—in other words, tools that help the GMs to position, launch and promote new products that make it all the way through the development and launch pipelines.

An often-used metric in such a business is the fraction of revenue being derived from new products as a percentage of the total revenues. For example, the business may define new products as products introduced in the prior 12 months on a rolling basis.

In Operational Excellence businesses, the emphasis is on the lowest total landed cost of the goods or services being delivered to the market. Such businesses are part of an ecosystem where business supply-chains compete with one another. Supply-chains control everything from strategic sourcing of material to the point past the actual, physical delivery to the customer; yes, beyond delivery to the immediate customer. Such businesses take an extended view of the supply chain. Their supply-chain costs acknowledge reverse supply-chains as well-customer rejects and their related costs. The net landed cost of products in such companies includes the cost of returns. The senior team in such businesses brings a relentless focus to bear on process quality, especially in the extended supply-chain process.

The Insightful CIO studies the extended supply chain in such businesses to understand the general flow of material, man-power and money; and also the flow of accompanying information. Armed with this understanding, the Insightful CIO explores methods to improve the fidelity and timeliness of information, so improve the fidelity and timeliness of information, so that the flow of material in the chain is uninterrupted. This understanding becomes the basis for her to make investment decisions and commit resources.

In such businesses, the Insightful CIO aligns herself with the heads of operations and supply-chain management. In an ideal situation, the CIO becomes a trusted partner of the people entrusted with managing the Cost of Goods Sold (COGS) line on the P&L. The CIO's charter in this relationship is to continually bring ideas to the table that can reduce the friction—costs embedded in the COGS line.

Companies focused on operational excellence use the quantified and measured reduction in COGS as a percentage of revenue in determining improvements. Alternately, they develop finely-granulated metrics that contribute to margins as a means to push for improvements.

In Customer Intimacy businesses, the emphasis is on delighting the customer. Such businesses exist in an ecosystem where customers perceive value above and significantly beyond a specific buy-sell transaction. Brand and brand-loyalty play an important role. Developing a customer-base and capturing a customer has a significant life-time value. Businesses focused on customer intimacy understand that a thorough understanding of the customer's pain and their own high quality of solutions are the price of entry, not a differentiator.

For example, Rockwell Automation (RA) provides solutions to automate complex manufacturing facilities, among other things. RA chooses to embed its own discrete hardware and software products in a basket of services. Based on customer desire, the basket can extend beyond RA's own products. When you think about it, if a manufacturing line is down for any reason, the specific reason is only of secondary interest. Of primary interest is restoring the manufacturing line to normalcy. RA often chooses to take a turn-key approach in such situations. It chooses to "own" the up-time of a manufacturing line, regardless of the source of the various elements that make up the line.

The Insightful CIO studies the broader business development process closely. This entails gaining a deep understanding of how potential markets are assessed, how new markets are developed; and how customers are acquired and retained. This understanding becomes the basis of strategic IT investment decisions.

The Insightful CIO becomes a trusted partner to both the CMO and the VP of Sales in such organizations. His charter in this relationship is to continually bring to the table strategies and tools that can accelerate the conversion of prospects to customers by offering information-rich products and services; and for IT-enabled mechanisms that create greater customer stickiness to the business.

Typically, there are three clear measures of success in such businesses. One is the number of new customers acquired in a given period of time. The second is the amount of business (measured as both revenue per customer and profits per customer, at the very least) garnered from existing customers in the same period. And the third is customer "churn" in that period—the "absolute" loss of customers from the customer base.

Are there other elements to the CIO's accountability? Of course, the foregoing discussion is merely meant to enable CEOs to better align and position the CIO. It is not meant to be an exhaustive listing of all the accountabilities of the CIO. Once the primary value discipline axis has been determined, the CIO should continue to make "good-enough" investments in other areas of the applications portfolio. The CIO should engage in a dialog with the senior team to make "at par" investments in such areas, so as not to cede ground to the competition and thereby, place the business at a relative disadvantage.

In addition to this, it is critical that IT infrastructure is adequately addressed. In many organizations, CIOs make needless investments in ensuring 7x24x365 infrastructure capabilities in ALL areas. Such capabilities come with both a very large up-front cost and a prohibitive recurring cost. As in the case of the applications portfolio, most entities can get along with "good enough" infrastructure that has 99.9% availability. This equates to roughly 500 minutes of published down-time in a year. And such capabilities cost a lot less than the 5-9s (or 99.999%) availability which is required in a rare few applications.

The CIO should be held accountable for better availability in infrastructure that supports the primary value discipline.

For instance, it makes total sense to invest heavily to get 5-9s for a value-chain application in a business focused on operational excellence. In such a business, a Customer Relationship Management (CRM) application may need just 2-9s (with 5000 minutes of downtime in a year).

Other elements of accountability for The Insightful CIO include the "need-to-play" elements in the IT portfolio— Operations, Quality Assurance and Program/ Project Management. These elements are common, no matter the value discipline of the business.

To whom should the CIO report?

This is a question that intrigues—and occasionally, vexes— many CEOs, while being of immense interest to all CIOs. And beware if you so much as ask an incumbent CIO this question! While there is definitely no absolutely "correct" answer, there are many "wrong" answers.

A question the CEO should ask himself while making this decision is, "Do we need our CIO to be a 'Transformative CIO'? Or are we seeking an 'Operational CIO'?" The answer will help sort through the possibilities of optimal alignment. It is also noteworthy that the answer can change as times change. The circumstances—and therefore, the needs—of an organization change with time, thus influencing the reporting relationship. This relationship is then more a reflection of the need of the organization than a commentary on the capability of the incumbent or the desires of the CEO.

By definition, a Transformative CIO is expected to "transform" some aspect of the business-maybe something that does not yet exist but that the CEO wants to bring in, perhaps something that is broken, or some aspect of the business that is suspect. The CEO could be contemplating a major thrust; and expects that doing so will tear apart the current fabric of the business. By taking preemptive measures, the CEO is attempting to ensure the successful outcome of his impending change initiative.

No matter the specific reason for such a transformation, the CIO is now an agent of change. Her arsenal of IT tools is being called upon to help the CEO achieve some business goals. Besides the usual weapons used by the CIO—people, processes, technological tools, metrics and incentive schemes-the 'Transformative CIO' now needs additional ammunition. The Insightful CIO realizes that she now possesses the "Magic Wand" of change; the clout to ask difficult questions; the authority to go where people have been hesitant to go before; the explicit permission to propose new perspectives that replace the dead logic of the past. In such an environment, the CIO must have the support of the CEO. Anything less than a direct reporting relationship with the CEO will render the CIO less potent in the world of real-politik.

If the answer to the CEO's question is that the organization needs an "Operational CIO," a CIO could align her role and expectations with the axis that best defines the operation of the organization. Her primary, if not preemptive, charter should be to add to the operational efficiencies and effectiveness of the organization.

The CIO is still an agent of change, but with a smaller sphere of influence. In such a case, her charter is to almost always look out for the axis that differentiates the business from the competition.

To use the flywheel metaphor, the CIO needs to add to the angular momentum constantly.

Let us review the problem of reporting alignment in the context of the value disciplines discussed previously.

In Product Leadership businesses, it is likely that there are many different business units, each with its unique set of IT needs, making it difficult for the CIO to report to a specific General Manager. Every GM will probably expect the CIO to report to his office.

One solution to such a situation is to explore whether the business has a higher-level organizational authority to whom all the GMs report—say, a Chief Development Officer, the President of the business, or a Chief Operating Officer. If such is the case, the CIO should report to this position. Doing so will help the business to derive optimal value from the CIO organization.

In Operational Excellence businesses, the CIO could report to whoever "owns" the COGS line on the P&L. If it is the Chief Operating officer, then the CIO could report to the COO.

In Customer Intimacy businesses, following the same logic, the CIO could report to the CMO or the VP of Sales.

In essence, the CIO should have a peer seat at the table where senior executives who "own" the business value-discipline discuss topics of significance. The CIO should be privy to the thoughts and concerns of all the senior executives who collectively share in this ownership. The consideration here is more than just posturing or titular. It is a seat at the highest organizational table where thorny problems surface, are discussed, and where the organization's resource allocation decisions are being made. Seated at the same table, the CIO is privy to all the interrelated value-discipline concerns. She is thus more capable of successfully partnering with and adding value to the business—to bring value to the table, to internalize business concerns, to address business needs in an appropriate time-frame.

An inappropriately aligned role will simply dilute the perceived value of the CIO function and eventually, the effectiveness of the CIO organization. A good CEO will take the time to carefully study her own direct report relationships and help the CIO to become structurally aligned appropriately.

How about reporting to the CFO?

In a significant fraction of organizations, CIOs report into the Chief Finance Officer or CFO. Such an arrangement has both historic and perceptual connotations. Historically speaking, in early applications, computerized information systems were deployed to automate drudge-work in the back-offices that dealt with day-to-day accounting. Work like time-card collation and payroll computation lent themselves admirably in this regard. Since these were in the CFO's domain, the Head of IT (or Electronic Data Processing, as it was then called) reported to the CFO. It made perfect sense to do so.

In today's world, CEOs entrust the organization's most valuable assets to be managed by their CFOs. One could argue that the organization's business data and information is significantly valuable. Therefore, by logical extension, one could continue to argue that the CFO—the CEO's chosen treasury guardsman—should have oversight responsibility over IT.

I feel that the question should be: Is this the best, the most strategic, alignment for the IT function in the organization? If the office of the CFO optimizes the opportunity for the CIO function to participate, contribute and impact the business, the answer, of course, is yes. While this may be the end-point, a thoughtful CEO will explore other possibilities carefully as a start-point first.

Ashwin Rangan

Summary

Great CEOs are interested in long-term enterprise value creation for the benefit of shareowners. To do so, they pick on a particular axis wherein their business shows promise. They then make investment choices that favor that axis. Good CIOs understand that providing automation and instrumentation in support of the business is their job. Insightful CIOs discover the CEO's axis of choice early. They then make IT investment decisions that disproportionately favor that axis. Over time, the chosen axis becomes a competitive differentiator. Insightful CIOs are comfortable with who they are. They are not defined by their reporting relationship within the business.

Insights and probes

1. A crucial first step for the CIO is to converse with the CEO and develop a clear underst anding of the value discipline of the business that she serves. What is your business's value-discipline?

Product Leadership? Operational Excellence? Customer Intimacy? Two of them at the same time? All three? Can't tell yet?

2. Through this dialog, the CIO should develop a holistic understanding of the critical areas—the value discipline areas, leveraging the business that deliver differentiated value to the customer, and so on. These should be the areas of focus for disproportionate IT investments on an accretive basis over a sustained period of time. Where are your "differentiable" investments in IT? For what period of time is this planned? How will you know when you get there?

3. The CIO should be held accountable to demonstrate that her organization is creating additional value along the business's primary value discipline. What is the metric you have devised to measure overall IT value-addition? Who measures it? How often is it measured? Is your compensation tied to the outcome of such a measurement?

4. The CIO's organization should also be measured for making investments for the other disciplines

that match the "average," from a competitive perspective-in other words, investments which are at-par. How do you benchmark your investments vis-à-vis the competition along the other axes?

5. The CEO should insure that the CIO reports to a position in the organization that best positions the CIO function for success. To whom do you report within the organization? Is this reporting relationship helpful in gaining the best possible alignment from a strategic view-point?

Mental modeling for the neophyte

1. You should develop your business understanding to the point that you can have informed dialogs with the CEO and other senior executives in the business vernacular. Do you possess these skills already? If not, perhaps you could engage a "retired CIO" as an executive coach. Or attend a senior leadership course focused on developing the business skills of CIOs.

2. How comfortable and confident are you when dealing

with senior executives? Are you nervous? Too slow for them? Too fast? Too verbose? Too cryptic, with many acronyms that tend to be technical? Can your executive summary in any area meet the "elevator test"? If you do not know the answers to these questions, ask the audience, whenever you get a chance. They will tell you. And if they share areas for improvement, take corrective action as soon as you can. Practice. And apply your new learnings to the old material. Iterate. Seek feedback.

3. Study the competition. Be sure to understand their business almost as well as you do your own business, if not better. "Keep your friends close; and your enemies closer." As much as you are an authority in your domain, you should be, or become, an expert in vividly describing your competition when asked. Read publications that detail your industry and chronicle your business space. Regularly.

Section 2: Finding friendship

"Synergies are something that the CEO basically has to force to happen, because organizations are, generally, like bodies in motion that tend to stay in motion. It's very hard to get big organizations to change. And it takes really a very powerful mandate to force things to happen."

John Malone,
Chairman of Liberty Media

Chapters 5 through 7 deal with the individual interaction of the CIO with other C-level executives in the enterprise who can most significantly impact the CIO function. In most businesses, these are the CFO and the COO, besides the CEO.

In theory, well-run businesses that show great financial results are highly synchronized machines. One imagines that the vision in such businesses is clear and shared; executive-level interactions are free and fluid; day-to-day realities meet preconceived expectations effortlessly and predictably. This is all in theory, of course.

In reality, if a business leader can identify that his organization needs a CIO, it is likely that the business is neither small nor simple. Even the best run businesses have the need to reiterate their vision for the benefit of their team-members. This is simply because realities intervene to overturn ideal theory and strategies carefully concocted at offsite meetings. Added to this, there is turn-over in both the rank-and-file and in the C-suite. New team-members bring in fresh new ideas and perspectives—sometimes, and perhaps rightly so, ideas that are orthogonal to the business' long-held vision and beliefs. Newness introduces awkwardness. Edges are rough. Cogs don't mesh. Over time, this awkwardness dissipates; but this is not always the case. Even as jagged edges persist, day-to-day realities force people to "just get-along," doing what they need to, to just keep the wheels turning. This creates some situations where expectations lack clarity or consistence, resulting in assumptions being made. Outcomes are not appropriately measured when and in the manner most suited to the occasion.

Enter the Insightful CIO, one of those rare senior executives who can interface and interact with every aspect of the business. Such a CIO understands that the success of the IT function is a reflection of the success of the business that he serves. He fundamentally "gets" alignment - that he should periodically synthesize his world-view with those of his colleagues, so that the integrity of the resulting gestalt is never compromised.

Good CIOs create opportunities to engage in dialog with their business partners regularly. Insightful CIOs go a step beyond. They create a framework that lubricates this interaction; with a framework that anticipates the agenda and "buckets" agenda elements ahead of time.

We will start this section with a chapter on how the Insightful CIO "buckets" his thoughts. We use this framework to frame discussion between the Insightful CIO and the CFO and the COO.

5. The CIO's Domain Is A Dog's Breakfast

"Computers shouldn't be unusable. You don't need to know how to work a telephone switch to make a phone call, or how to use the Hoover Dam to take a shower, or how to work a nuclear-power plant to turn on the lights."

Scott McNealy
Co-Founder of Sun Microsystems

A CIO's primary goal is to align the IT function with the business; and to manage a portfolio of IT assets in response to the needs of the business strategy. Ideally, this portfolio provides the business with an information technology infrastructure, transactional capabilities, information to support decision-making and, in the most advanced cases, a strategic business advantage.

We could assume that the business and IT talk—that they discuss areas of concern regularly, and use a shared vocabulary. We could also assume that the business has a strategy that is clearly thought-out and well articulated, and further that the IT function has sufficient resources (talent, time and money) to supply and sustain a portfolio of capabilities to the business that creates a competitive advantage.

All CIOs would like to believe that they do a good job in this, and definitely do their best, day after day, occasionally seeking validation from their colleagues. The Insightful CIO is by definition a careful planner. He plans for alignment and achieves it. Through well-implemented processes, he manages expectations, measures and maintains alignment over time and transparently reports on it.

Focus planning on the business? Or on technology? Or both?

An often asked question goes as follows: Should the CIO focus on the business and make IT decisions in response? Or should he instead focus on Technology and present its business benefits to his business colleagues?

I would recommend the third option—both—with a clear bias towards the business. In fact, that's what sets the Insightful CIO apart. Insightful CIOs runs the IT function as though it were a business by itself. Rather than treat IT as a cost-center, he creates externally-focused processes that enable IT value-delivery to "stakeholders"—the business that IT serves. He creates metrics and measures that clearly shows how IT is aligned with the business. He creates mechanisms to measure and publishes results of IT's performance. Collaborating with his senior team peers, he co-creates mechanisms that ensure objectivity and transparency. In this, he invites scrutiny and feedback—just as a well-run stand-alone business serves up information for scrutiny by its stakeholders.

Let us recall the definition of a business: as the relentless pursuit of a set of core business processes, repeated to maximize value for the paying customer, thereby creating enterprise value for the benefit of the shareholders. Treating his function as a business, the Insightful CIO demands that his function is reviewed and assessed with the same microscope that is used to assess a well-scrutinized, publicly-traded business. If indeed his offerings are above-board, not only is there nothing to hide, but in fact, there is reason for the Insightful CIO to be proud. Once the CIO organization achieves such an alignment and transparency, success lies in continually assembling appropriate IT-enabled assets and capabilities. The CIO should now showcase such investments. Doing so, he can continually and proudly prove that IT investments reduce the friction of defining, developing and delivering business value to the paying customer.

A pyramid of possibilities

Let us start with an understanding of businesses processes. Business processes are tasks done and steps taken by people in the business to get a business transaction "conducted" through the organization. In a sense, it is like hand-holding a child through a seemingly bewildering labyrinth, when viewed from the outside-in. Information systems seek to "hard-wire" these business transactions so that they are "conducted" through the organization faster. In this sense, Information Technology systems merely "express" these business processes, using abstractions and symbols. A good portfolio of IT investments is a combination of infrastructural, transactional, informational and strategic components, in support of the organization's business processes. Viewed as a pyramid of possible IT capabilities, infrastructural components spread out the base, followed by transactional components next up, then informational components, and strategic components at the top.

As its position in the pyramid suggests, infrastructural components are foundational. They serve to provide basic utility-like capabilities. They play a critical role—in that, when businesses demand or claim to be "infinitely scalable," their IT foundation is the determinant of such a claim. Since they constitute the foundational layer, they have to be rock-solid and available, no matter the load placed on them.

To cite an analogy, imagine the system of roads and traffic lights in transportation: they do not have a function in and as of themselves, but serve to carry and regulate traffic. Similarly, infrastructure elements enable the other activities in CIO organizations and help regulate "data traffic." Like vehicular traffic, IT infrastructure is most noticed when there are "traffic jams."

Transaction components deal with primitive data—data acquisition, data processing and data storage. Timeliness, completeness and integrity govern the adequacy of technologies at this level.

Informational components are derivatives built from data that is already captured and stored in the transactional layer. In effect, information is processed data. Information assists the business in answering decision-making, responding to questions that begin with "what," "who," "when" and "where."

At the apex of the pyramid are strategic components. These components are a combination of external and internal sources of information, and assist the business with existential questions, responding to questions that look outward and inward. They typically help the business respond to questions that begin with "how" and "why."

It is noteworthy that "structured" transactional data typically represents less than a third of information in most organizations. Not only is unstructured data the majority; it is also the faster growing segment of the two. We will look at these in greater detail in a following section.

An increasingly compelling backdrop to the pyramid

Business has always been a balancing act—between risks and rewards, a tug-of-war between what are permissible and prudent. The definitions of permissibility and prudence have become the warp and weft of an increasingly compelling trend in recent times. The internal complexity of conducting daily business, especially in the United States, has become intertwined with statutes and regulations imposed on the conduct of business.

While fair trade practices demanded transparency, and open markets controlled by the rule of the law assured market participants that they could expect their just-rewards to be protected, businesses have historically exploited asymmetries and loop-holes in the framework of the law.

The net result of all of these thrusts and parries is an increasingly complex body of law that prescribes statutory and regulatory disclosures. Regardless of the pedigree of these laws, rules and practices, they are meant to help businesses reduce, mitigate and manage risks. Most of the time, they indeed do so, especially when viewed in isolation. However, when viewed in whole, business laws and regulatory oversight can be a bewildering maze, especially in large organizations.

Some of these regulations apply to all businesses, whether small or large. A good example here is the

Payment Card Industry, or PCI, rules. The PCI Security Standards Council is an open global forum for the ongoing development, enhancement, storage, dissemination and implementation of security standards for payment account data protection. Whether the business is Wal-Mart or a mom-and-pop retail outlet, protecting both the privacy of an individual and enabling a secure environment for that individual to conduct a credit card transaction fosters better business. The PCI guidelines and rules define such an environment.

Other rules and laws apply to all businesses in a given industry vertical, for both public and private enterprises. An excellent example in this category is the Health Insurance Portability and Accountability Act, or HIPAA, rules. HIPAA applies to health plans, health care clearinghouses and to any health care provider, however large or small, who transmits health information in electronic form. So whether you are a Kaiser Permanente Healthcare System, or you are "Doc" Jenkins down the street, if you even transmit so much as a byte of healthcare information electronically, you are liable to be subject to HIPAA regulations.

Yet others apply only to publicly traded businesses.

In recent memory, the most famous of them is the Sarbanes-Oxley Act, also called Sarb-Ox or SOX. More formally, it is known as the Public Company Accounting Reform and Investor Protection Act of 2002. SOX was passed in response to a number of major corporate and accounting scandals in the late 1990s and the early 2000s, including those affecting Enron, Tyco International, and WorldCom. These scandals eroded the public trust in accounting and reporting practices. The legislation—not surprisingly—is wide ranging and establishes new or enhanced standards for all U.S. public company boards, management, and public

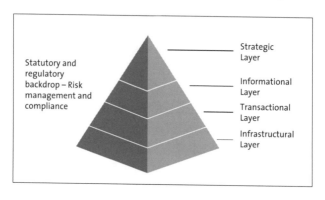

Figure 5.1 - A pyramid of possibilities

Ashwin Rangan

accounting firms. As with other regulations that are not indexed to size, SOX applies to ExxonMobil as much as it does to the most recently floated business on any one of the US Boards.

Besides what is permissible within statutory and regulatory laws, there is the aspect of business prudence. As a business, are we taking enough risks? Are we concurrently taking appropriate steps to mitigate and manage risks? Are our practices supportive of business continuity, if an 8.0 earthquake were to level our home-office facility tomorrow? Are the most important differentiators in our business—the secret sauce that makes us who we are—well protected? That's the intellectual property, or IP, that creates leverage for us. IT security and privacy play a key role in defining, developing and implementing these measures.

The foundation layer of the pyramid in CIO organizations

In its infancy, and in its most primitive form, technology infrastructure was the name of the CIO game—pipes, speeds and feeds. The CIO was required to provide the business with compute power, data storage capacity, connectivity and networking.

Today, these continue to be the building blocks that enable anything greater in value-add. Just their presence does not add value. However, their absence detracts from the value proposition immediately and noticeably.

Studying an analogy clarifies this quickly. In the electric power utilities space, technology infrastructure is the equivalent of the power generation plant's distribution infrastructure. In and as of themselves, they do not create value; but most industries cannot function without an uninterrupted supply of electric power. In this, the users of the electricity grid infrastructure are creating a derivative product. So much so that when there is a power failure, the impact is both immediate and noticeable.

To get optimal results with infrastructure takes a deep understanding of elemental interplay. Particularly when the scale and complexity of infrastructure become appreciable, laws of physics and applied mathematics become applicable. To comprehend and leverage this increasingly complex and sophisticated, not to mention expensive, domain in IT, a titular head—the CTO or Chief

Technology Officer—has emerged. This is especially true in organizations with complex IT infrastructure, many of which are also large businesses.

Good CTOs are informed by the business and its imperatives. Once the infrastructure is commissioned, it needs to remain a well-managed environment that is always available. Continuing to use the analogy of the electric power utilities, the power grid must be monitored, measured and periodically upgraded for both better capability (technology advancement—from copper wires to aluminum cables, for example, in the transmission environment; or from coal-fired generators to green-and-clean gas generators in the power generation environment) and capacity (demand). In almost all CIO organizations, a Head of Operations has emerged to own the accountability for this aspect of infrastructure management. The label varies. Head of IT Infrastructure or the Head of IT Operations are a couple of the more common and frequently favored titles.

The second layer of the pyramid in CIO organizations

At the next level up from infrastructure is elemental data or transaction processing. The goal here is to capture business-relevant data fully and accurately and to process it—capturing data, storing it and ensuring that related data elements are linked in such a fashion that interrelated data can be relatively easily retrieved.

As easy as this may look, it took a couple of decades of intense work by tens of thousands of technology professionals to advance these capabilities. The results are what we today call database management capabilities.

Data is an abstraction of the real world, and not surprisingly, this problem has manifold dimensions. The teams tasked with making sense from data have had to codify the abstractions, and technology vendors in turn have had to create and provide capabilities to manipulate and store these abstractions. Data capture and manipulation capabilities—also called programming languages—went through many iterations.

So did efficient data storage and linking capabilities —i.e., database technologies.

Imagine a basketball team, one that has been playing for a number of years—say the LA Lakers. Transaction processing can be likened to score-keeping for the Lakers—collecting, collating and reporting basic statistics. Based on such scores, a student of the Lakers can quickly tell that the Lakers started out as a Minneapolis team, reel off the names and jersey numbers of the Lakers over the years, the schedules and scores of the team, wins and losses, over-time statistics and so on.

Good CIO organizations today have teams that commission and manage these elements of the information technology function. Typical titles reflective of these capabilities in the CIO organization are Head of Transaction Processing Services and Head of ERP Services. Over time, the enablers of these capabilities—the required hardware and software—have become standardized and readily available, so much so that commoditization is the trend at these layers of the pyramid. As with all commodities, unit cost of end-to-end transaction processing is the driver from a business point of view.

The third layer of the pyramid in CIO organizations

Moving up to the next layer in our notional pyramid, CIO organizations create and provision informational components to the business. Information is a derivative of stored data that is further manipulated and

transformed to re-represent it, but at a higher level of abstraction. An entire new industry in information technology emerged to enable businesses to leverage this space, variously called data-warehousing, data-marting, business intelligence, business analytics and so on. Tools and technologies, both in hardware and software, have evolved to support and advance this sub-domain, where the business promise is the ability to "boil the ocean" of data and extract hidden insights.

To continue with our analogy of a basketball team, analyzing the Lakers' historic trend reveals that they win over half their home games—a fact derived from information related to games. This is not inherently intrinsic to any game played by the Lakers. Instead, this is data about data, or meta-data, in the argot of the trade. This is insight that is not readily visible. It is a derivative from the underlying transactional data. It is becoming common to see dedicated teams within CIO organizations addressing this area. There is no convergence in terms of title, but it is clear that the area is a creative one—even in the title assigned to the head of this area!

The apex of the pyramid in CIO organizations

And finally, at the top of the pyramid, we have information and insights that are derived from both transactional data and the first-order derivatives inferred from them. This is where CIO organizations deal with strategic information technology components. There are a few points worth noting here.The value of derivatives is only as good as the integrity of the underlying components. In other words, if the quality, timeliness, cleanliness and reliability of basic data are questionable, information that is derived from such data is inherently *worth less*. Not worthless, but just less valuable. If the data collection and collation process proves suspect—even once—it introduces an element of doubt, where there may have been none before.

It is also worth noting that strategy is a fluid state in business. There are few elements of business that remain strategic for extended periods of time. If one definition of business strategy is its game plan, the game plan should morph and change as the situation changes and the competition makes its moves.

A CIO should consider these two trains of thoughts even as she plans out her portfolio of strategic components. The organizational arm that is building and managing strategic information assets should have a data-integrity assurance arm. Both the CIO organization and the business should understand that the strategic components will change, reflective of the changing needs of the business.

It is worth examining these thoughts further, extending the analogy of the LA Lakers basketball team. Historically, the Lakers have always been in play-offs when the win-to-loss ratio has been better than 65 percent. Lower, in fact; but 65% assures them of a berth without a question. To understand and forecast if the team will make it to the play-offs, the team has to just track this average. However, this average is in turn influenced by the outcome of every game played by the Lakers in a given season, which, in turn, is based on every basket scored by every player in every game, both in the Lakers team and in the opposition.

Assuming that the Lakers are headed towards the play-offs, it is reasonable to assume that some other team is also headed there to face them. It is very likely that the team that will face them is different every time. And even more so that the players on that team are different from the last time they were in the play-offs. A strategic component of an information system supporting the Lakers could be a video library that shows the behavior of the opposition players during games and play-offs; ideally, against the Lakers themselves. Clearly, the contents of the library have to change, depending on the opposite team.

Even the best of businesses is only just beginning to realize the value of such dynamically configured strategic components. Commissioning such components is expensive. Businesses are hard-pressed to justify such expenses, especially when the asset may not have value beyond short-term engagements. Data-intensive businesses are at the vanguard of such strategic investments—businesses like online retail banking, financial services, insurance businesses and so on. In the domain of information provisioning and business analytics, both hardware and software offerings are showing early signs of standardization. It is early days, yet, and if history is an indicator, this could take a decade or more to sort itself out.

There are no standard offerings in the area of strategic information assets. Even leading-edge businesses appear to be at an experimental stage, where they have to measure and confirm the value of their investments for the benefit of the business. More success stories in this regard will help more businesses conceptualize such asset builds.

Both the sub-domains of business analytics and of strategic enablement create real, measurable, differentiated value to the business. New and different measurement techniques and new metrics are required to adequately quantify the ROI in these emergent areas of IT.

Extending the basic framework

Beyond these basic layers of the pyramid, good CIO organizations embrace other framework facets to serve the business. There are 3 elements that I have used in the course of my career.

Ashwin Rangan

First and foremost, good CIO Organizations invest in a strong Quality Assurance sub-domain. No matter the layer at which additional assets are being developed or deployed, given the pervasive—and often undocumented—nature of enabling information technology components, a QA component is a relatively small investment to make when compared to either the investment or the expected returns on investment.

Well-established CIO organizations today have pathways providing access to scalable, repeatable Quality Assurance. This is like Risk Mitigation 101. However, it is note-worthy that not all CIO organizations invest in even this basic layer of risk-management.

Then, good CIO organizations invest in Relationship Management. This is a competency that, over time, enables the CIO organization to develop a good and lasting relationship with its customer-base. In doing so, great CIO organizations are able to proactively sniff out business needs long before they are formally articulated and spelled out as requirements. This gives the IT organizations more time to react when they are formally requested to help. Insightful CIO organizations deploy Program / Project Management as a value-added element, tagging these abilities right behind Relationship Management. Program Management becomes the delivery arm of the concepts explored, developed and specified by the Relationship Management team members.

Finally, some CIO organizations have established an arm that is specifically designed for and aimed toward business process re-engineering (BPR). This was in vogue briefly for about 5 or 6 years in the early 1990s. It then fell out of favor, but seems to be on a road to recovery. As organizational complexity increases, processes tend to become codified. This is good. However, with time, they become calcified, cementing organizational behaviors in place. Quite often, the reason to change becomes somewhat diffusely obvious. The old process does not seem to work any more. A clear and early sign is when variations to the defined process—so called exceptions—start to number in the double-digits. Some one in the organization typically recognizes that the business is headed towards a tipping-point, beyond which processes have to be re-assessed and re-designed. Unfortunately, organizational lethargy and inertia is the dark-side of process re-design and re-definition. BPR activities in leading-edge businesses focus on such calcified processes and change processes to reflect new realities. Much has been written about BPR over the years. For me, Hammer and Champy's Reengineering the Corporation continues to be the seminal work in this regard.

Of these three activities, QA services are increasingly better understood. Specialty houses focused on IT QA offer a list of services, and given this trend toward commoditization, QA should be managed to drive-down unit costs.

Relationship Management and BPR are both sub-domains that require in-depth knowledge of the organization and its processes. They require a level of understanding of the business that usually takes years to gain. The Insightful CIO understands that constantly seeking value-based BPR initiatives is a high value-add functions in the CIO organization. In course of time, these services are the differentiated offerings from such a CIO organization.

Core versus Context in the CIO organization

Geoff Moore introduced the concepts of core and context a few years ago. Context refers to those business activities that must be performed just to remain in business; not necessarily to deliver differentiated value to the customer. By contrast, core refers to business activities that directly create or deliver unique and differentiated value to the customer. These are the activities which prompts a possible prospect to become a raving fan of the business.

Core and context are both conceptual. They exist in a fluid continuum. What is core today could become context tomorrow. It is rare to see the reverse occur. However, it is possible to imagine that new "cores" can and will emerge with the passage of time.

For example, when PCs were new in the early 1980s in the CIO organizations, just placing a newly procured PC on a desktop and getting it to operate was enough differentiation. It was core. This was when desktop productivity applications were first introduced.

As yesterday's leading edge has become today's mainstream, yesterday's core has become today's context. The point here is that CIOs should carefully assess their service offerings periodically, and classify activities as core or context dispassionately.

After binning out IT services as one or the other, context should be managed for unit-cost of delivery. These are activities that naturally lend themselves to outsourcing, if not both off-shoring and outsourcing. CIOs should remember that these are activities that do not create or deliver differentiated customer value.

In direct contrast, core activities should be revered as though they are the crown-jewels being offered to paying customers. As with crown-jewels, the core should sparkle when offered. Core offerings should be branded and positioned; their differentiated value proposition should be clearly articulated in business terms. Example use-cases should be developed in anticipation, wherein explanations are couched in terms that the intended business audience will understand.

In closing this section of the chapter, I will submit that in great CIO organizations, there is brilliant clarity in the services catalog between core and context.

Your own world-view

As individuals, we all have points-of-view that are unique. These views form the basis of our world-view. Let me clarify that I am not talking about personality traits here. I refer to the unique bias with which we each of us tend to see the world. This view tints our perceptions and actions daily. 2 X 2 matrices are often leveraged by practitioners to study and better understand the interplay of 2 sets of 2 variables each, wherein each set seeks to define a terminal point in a spectrum of possibilities. Consultants are often teased about their world-view being defined by 2 X 2 matrices. While being clichéd, matrix frameworks do help in collating and bucketing a set of orthogonal but inter-related variables.

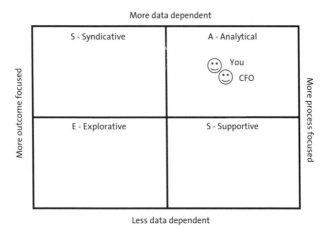

Figure 5.2 - The ASsESs matrix of natural tendency

Ashwin Rangan

Early in my career, I was exposed to such a 2 x 2 framework to help assess and peg my colleagues' perspectives. I found this matrix to be valuable in helping me understand the various points-of-view of people around me. Unlike some of the more advanced or better known behavioral frameworks, this framework is not finely granulated. Nonetheless, it gives me a "roughly-right" clue to the world-view of people with whom I interact.

The first goal here is to find your positional fix on this grid. This is more difficult than you may at first imagine. The reason, of course, is that, if you are like me, you will have a tendency to look at yourself with rose-tinted glasses when doing a self-assessment.

However, there is a relatively easy way to get a good read on your fix. It is to share this framework with a few trusted advisors first. Explain the meaning of the two axes. In order for you to get grounded on your own fix, it is only necessary for you to explain the axes with the same rigor—however clearly or coarsely—to each of your trusted advisors. Request them to provide individual and independent feedback to you. Where do they see your 'fix' on the grid? Independently and concurrently, plot your position as you see it, and as objectively as you can. With a few, easy interactions, you will spiral down to a spot that best plots your position. The wisdom of your trusted group will usually place you in roughly the right quadrant, although specific plot-points may be scattered. Some plot-points may even be on a different side of the axes relative to others, but a strong quadrant will emerge as a common theme.

So, in a sense, this is a perceptual personality grid. Using "roughly right" language, it will inform you if your world-view is Analytical, Supportive, Explorative or, to define a new word, Syndicative.

As shown in the figure, our 2x2 matrix has 4 quadrants. The X-axis considers a bias to action while the Y-axis considers a bias to data. The quadrants are labeled Analyst, Supporter, Explorer or Syndicator. The gentleman who introduced me to this framework jokingly remarked that it makes ASsESs of all of us—referring to the first four letters of the quadrants. I smile whenever I remember that particular conversation. Nonetheless, it helps me to remember the framework easily and also to classify others quickly. ASSES indeed!

To be sure, one could be anywhere on this 2 X 2 matrix and be good at what they do. As I said before, this is about how you see the world and how the world sees you. This in no way is meant to either judge your capabilities or pigeon-hole your skills. In this, it informs you of likely inherent biases. It does not validate or invalidate your point of view- it simply informs you about the dynamics of your own interaction with others. A critical first step to synthesizing a world-view with colleagues is to first plot your own vantage point. So before you start engaging with your peers to create a shared worldview or "gestalt," it is a good idea to plot your own fix on this grid.

I will use this framework repeatedly for discussions in later chapters.

Summary

The CIO organization exists to support the business. In doing so, there are many different layers of information technology that the CIO makes available to the business. These technologies have inherent risks associated with them. Good CIOs create mechanisms to manage and mitigate IT-induced business risks. Insightful CIOs partner with the business to help re-engineer and transform the business, while remaining cognizant of IT-induced risks. They also know how to differentiate between technologies and capabilities that merit outsourcing versus those that demand to remain in-house. Finally, Insightful CIOs are active in first understanding their own world-view and then, in forging a strong, joint world-view with their executive colleagues.

Insights and probes

1. World-views are the result of synthesizing other people's perspectives with your own. They are not a still photograph, but are more like a long video. In this, they emerge and evolve. How well are you aligned with the business? Do you sense a shared gestalt? How often do you meet with your senior colleagues? Do you confirm alignment with them, when you do meet? What is on the agenda when you meet?

2. The CIO domain is complex, with many layers to

it. How have you explained this complexity to the business? Have you created a list of services that you offer your customers? Internal - as in facing your fellow-associates in the business? Or external - as in the ultimate, "paying customer"?

3. Not all CIO organizations undertake all of the functions described in this chapter. How does your "pyramid of offerings" stack up? Do you have extensions to the pyramid? What are they?

4. Like the business itself, IT has a core set of offerings and a context to such a core. In assessing your organization's offerings, do you differentiate between IT's core offerings and the contextual offerings?

5. To paraphrase Yogi Berra, "if you don't know where you are going, you will land up somewhere else." So it is important to know your location and speed, at all times. Does your organization measure and report differently on these two components—core and context—in terms of the specific location, speed and rate of change associated with that specific technology?

Mental modeling for the neophyte

1. When did you last discuss the dynamics of the business that you serve with your superior? Or with the business owners?

2. If you don't already have one, get yourself a mentor in the business segment that most interests you. Make it a point to meet with your mentor periodically. Prepare an agenda that helps you fill-in-the-gaps. Ideally, the agenda should reflect areas of interest to you and knowledge for your mentor.

3. In the pyramid of offerings, do you understand all the layers? Assess your level of understanding on one axis and competence on another axis. Be objective in this assessment. How do you plan to improve either your knowledge or your skills in the areas where you fall short? These should be the guideposts for your next developmental discussion with your supervisor or mentor or both.

4. How well do you understand the extensions to the concept of the pyramid—QA, Project management

and BPR? These are building blocks which the aspiring CIO should understand. As with the layers in the pyramid, think of strategies to assess your strengths and plans to shore-up your weaknesses.

5. Have a conversation with your business mentor about core and context. Create a mind-map of your thoughts about this differentiation and division. Then, use this as a guide to have a discussion with your mentor or a well-meaning colleague. Did you see eye to eye? If there were differences, what was the basis for them?

6. Using the ASsESs grid, request your peers and your supervisor to help you find your point-of-view. Pick someone from this same group with whom you don't always see eye to eye. Where would you plot that person? Is their plot-point different from yours? What does this tell you?

6. Out-Numbering The Numbers Man

"When you've got a CFO who is a business person and a CIO who is a technology person—and they don't live in each other's world—clash is inevitable. There needs to be fusion between these two strategic positions, or IT projects will fail."

Don Schulman
Global leader of financial management solutions
at IBM Business Consulting Services

In many ways, the relationship between Chief Financial Officers (CFOs) and CIOs is more special than the relationship between the CIO and any of his other peers. CFOs are guardians of cost-effective value-creation and delivery, while CIOs are stewards

Ashwin Rangan

of the application of appropriate technology to ensure efficient value-creation and delivery. Neither of them is actually responsible directly for business value-creation and delivery, but they are both integral to the process. In this, their goals are perfectly aligned; but their perspectives are not necessarily the same.

The CFO's world-view is largely concerned with cost-effectiveness; and the Insightful CIO's world-view is largely denominated by efficiencies. Neither of them can be successful without the other's perspective and the business needs both. Developing a common point-of-view and maintaining this perspective is challenging, but no different from the challenge that is faced by any two other critical functions in a business. To help this process, the CIO is well-advised to first study and understand the world from a CFO's perspective; assess the quadrant of the CFO's world-view; and finally, create and exercise processes to gain commonality and stay aligned.

Understanding the CFO organization

A CFO's charter is to create and present an abstraction of the on-going realities of the business in a clear, repeatable, and consistent format. In doing this over the centuries,

CFOs have evolved a set of tools to gain visibility into the business activity reliably. Needless to say, their chosen language is numbers.

The beauty of the CFO world is the manner in which they, as a body, have codified their domain— over time, with patience and persistence. They have made this codified body of knowledge an integral part of learning to do business; in fact, "learning business" is almost always synonymous with "learning the basics of Finance."

The CFO's basic business tools are the Balance Sheet, the Profit and Loss Statement (also called Income Statement or the P&L) and the Cash Flow statement. These traditional tools have many variables, and almost any business transaction involving money impacts one of these tools. CFOs need the means to capture every transaction detail accurately and in a timely fashion. To do so, they need systems.

Balance Sheets and P&L statements are like the rear-view mirrors of a car. They reflect activities in and up to a prior period, whether it is up to the last completed minute or reflective of last year's activities. CFOs create and leverage other instruments to understand the future in terms of financial impact. These include the Budget and assorted Net Present Value (NPV), Discounted Cash Flow (DCF), Internal Rate of Return (IRR) and Return on Investment (ROI) frameworks. In many cases, CFO organizations are also chartered with driving business analytics and decision support in the broader context of the business. At a deeper level, progressive CFO organizations need help the business unit completely understand the impact of IT.

In mature businesses, with well-aligned IT practices, CFO organizations work with the CIO organization and with the business units to create and exercise portfolio planning and management tools to insure on-going visibility into IT investments. CFOs are also responsible to measure, manage, mitigate, and report business risks. In this, they are not only accounting for business activities. In a sense, they are also being tasked as the Chief Accountability Officer in the organization. Related to this, they are tasked to build, verify and manage compliance with statutory and regulatory rules and requirements. CFOs typically use auditing tools, employing external and internal auditors in order to test for and ensure compliance.

Prelude to a dialog between the CFO and the CIO

CFOs work in a world that is driven by regular periodicity. In publicly-traded companies, the CFO typically has an annual cycle for planning and budgeting, a quarterly cycle, perhaps, when business results are reviewed and analyzed in the context of the budget, and a monthly cycle when the Balance Sheet and P&L are cast and shared with the leadership teams.

Besides these "periodic" activities, CFOs in publicly traded companies are required by law to file quarterly and annual financial results.

Additionally, in well-regulated free-market economies, such as the U.S., they are required to follow rules such as Reg FD (Regulatory Full Disclosure), whereby all financially "material" events have to be fully disclosed to the open market within 48 hours. Customarily, the "materiality" bar is set when variances exceed 2 percent of whatever is promised to be measured and reported within a given period.

The CIO should become conversant with regulatory "filings" and their time-sensitivity. His team should then sign-up to enable such activities by empowering the CFO with the most appropriate Information Technologies.

The Insightful CIO is familiar with the frameworks that most intimately impact the business that his team and he serve. In contrast to the CFO organization that works with clear, well-defined frequency, CIO organizations work in a world that is driven by projects and project-governance processes. There is no definite periodicity to this world. The CIO has a choice to overlay a time-driven process on top of an event-driven environment. CIOs who have a technical pedigree may not have a great deal of experience in understanding the CFO's tools and jargon. Since Finance is the language of business, CIOs who can understand this language—and who take it upon themselves to learn this—will experience returns beyond just interesting conversations with the CFO and his team.

Hypothesis of the CFO's world-view

In my experience, CFOs have come in one of three packages and I must say I have worked with about a dozen of them in the course of my business career until now.

In the next couple of sentences, I risk projecting my experience to extend and capture the whole CFO genre. The vast majority of CFOs—I would put this at over 65 percent—are traditional in their approach. They care about the P&L. They nag at the big spenders. They are conscientious about the details, to the point of being worry-warts.

A significant second segment of CFOs—in the 25 percent range—are less traditional. To them, the P&L is just another major contributor to the Balance Sheet. They are focused on leveraging the Balance Sheet, they worry about how, when and where to raise money or retire debts. They review debt versus equity constantly, and typically hire Controllers to keep a close watch on the P&L.

The third and last kind of CFO—those in the remaining 10 percent—are the most adventure-some.

These CFOs enjoy close encounters of the "deal" kind the most, where they lead the business in deal-making and deal-handling. In many ways, these CFOs could just as easily have been investment bankers themselves, but choose to serve a business from the inside instead. They operate at their peak capacities when they are in the thick of deal-making.

Regardless of the kind they are, these CFOs are always superb at numbers. It is almost as if numbers speak to them in a special, private language! If we were to use the 2 x 2 world-view grid from the last chapter, it is likely that the CFO's world-view is Analytical. Many, if not most, CFOs come from a background of having been Financial Analysts themselves. As the very name indicates, Analysts abstract data about events, organize them, and create a virtual picture of the proceedings.

As a core entity that measures and monitors the health of the business, the CFO organization is expected to deliver its work product as an input to other arms of the organization—whether they are Budgets, Income Statements, Balance Sheets or Plan versus Actual analyses. The expectation of the CFO organization is that it provides these financial pictures consistently, with a pre-determined frequency and with high integrity. CFO organizations thus tend to be data-oriented and process-centric. Good CFOs will likely be products of their circumstances—comfortable and confident when presented with data and confronted by process.

The Insightful CIO validates the exact position of the CFO using these hypotheses. Plotting the CFO and understanding the position of the plot-point vis-à-vis your own will help you understand where there may be cause for concern.

Meshing the world-views of the CFO and the CIO

One possible starting point for a dialog between the CFO and CIO is the pyramid discussed in Chapter 4. Using the pyramid as the basis for discussion creates a common reference framework.

A common thought framework is necessary in order to mesh world-views effectively. First, the CFO is a customer to the CIO, quite like any other member of the C-suite. The CFO needs IT-enabled tools to ensure that his organization delivers friction-free value to the business.

The CFO is very likely to be interested in risk management and compliance, and since his world is transaction-intensive, this too will be an area of interest. Tools critical to his function's success rely on high-quality data processing and information.

In addition to these topics of interest to the CFO, the Insightful CIO brings a couple of other items that

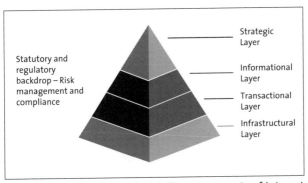

Figure 6.2 - The IT Pyramid with the components of interest to the CFO shaded

are of significant interest to himself to the table. These include:

- A means to jointly manage the applications portfolio for the enterprise;
- Initiatives sponsored by the CIO organization.
- IT finances.

A healthy discussion between CFOs and CIOs has at least the following five items on the agenda. There may be more, depending upon the specific roles of these two C-level colleagues. However, these five should serve as thought-starters in meshing the world-views of these two C-level executives.

Risk management and regulatory compliance

The Insightful CIO should initiate a discussion with the CFO about the enterprise's statutory and regulatory compliance. Every industry in the developed and developing world today has a set of explicit or implicit expectations in this regard. The CFO is typically the business sponsor for compliance. The adequacy or lack thereof of IT systems and controls can often substantially impact the outcome of compliance audits.

While the CFO may be responsible for compliance, the CFO organization is not usually the exclusive owner for all compliance-related data. A good item on such a discussion agenda should include plans to clearly identify other functional organizations that should be co-opted for driving compliance activities; setting priorities with these colleagues jointly; and creating dashboards to provide transparency regarding progress and ROI, if any, on such investments.

Most organizations dismiss compliance as a "cost of doing business." A few have embraced transparency and compliance as a means to embellish corporate lustre. The Insightful CIO engages his C-suite colleagues to find ways to shift their perspectives from the former to the latter point of view.

The CFO's tools and kits

The next agenda item should focus on the tools most often used within the CFO organization. The Insightful

CIO and CFO engage in a dialog to discuss whether the CFO organization has the necessary information technologies to capture and massage data that leads to the timely creation of the business Balance Sheet and P&L statements; and whether the CFO organization has the right Planning and Budgeting tools. In this segment of discussion, the CFO organization is both the data owner and the business sponsor.

Business initiatives, portfolio visibility, and expected ROI

The third item on the discussion agenda should be to review initiatives that are driven by, and impact the business. The business itself is the sponsor of such initiatives, and usually, the same segment that sponsors the initiative is the primary data-owner as well. Both the CFO and the CIO are enablers in these initiatives.

CFOs and CIOs may choose several tools to create and leverage portfolio visibility and management that also help them stay aligned, depending on the complexity of the business. Based on the required IT sophistication pertaining to the initiative, this may be either at the informational or the strategic level of the pyramid. The important point here is to ensure that the organization has a transparent mechanism to slot, view, fund, and manage IT initiatives as part of a portfolio, with a view to ultimately manage the ROI.

CIO-sponsored initiatives

The fourth item on the agenda should be a review of initiatives that are driven by the CIO organization itself. The CIO is the sponsor of such initiatives, and typically, these initiatives are technology-intensive. The CIO organization is both the data owner and the beneficiary of such initiatives. Such initiatives typically tend to be at the infrastructural level of the pyramid, heavily relying on the use of TLAs—Three Letter Acronyms—that telegraph the benefits to the technically-savvy, but are difficult, at best, to understand for any audience that is not technically proficient.

In the spirit of transparency, the Insightful CIO should spell out the costs and benefits of such initiatives.

These initiatives should also be a part of the shared portfolio of IT activities.

IT Financials

Finally, the fifth item on the agenda should be Financials in the context of the CIO organization. This segment of discussion should include at least three sub-sections: Capital Expenditures (CapEx), Operating Expenditures (OpEx) and Cost-per-unit-of-delivery metrics for contextual CIO organization activities.

Creating transparency: An approach to Portfolio Management

While I started out doubting whether transparency could at all be created for IT and IT-enablement initiatives, my philosophy has changed and evolved over the years. Today, I embrace transparency as a starting requirement for the successful engagement and alignment of IT with business. An organization-wide IT initiatives portfolio has proven vital in creating such transparency.

I am big on portfolio management, without being hung-up on a specific portfolio management approach or theory. There are many different theories and approaches to this important topic. Personally, I favor simple frameworks. In creating and refining the following framework over the years, I have arrived at four specific assumptions and conclusions.

First—and this realization took time—I realized that measuring and reporting took time and effort; an overhead activity in a project-driven IT organization. So I concluded that not all initiatives merit being measured or reported. I have also concluded that only the core initiatives in IT require this level of transparency, and even within that subset, I have set the low-bar at 150 person-hours. My thinking here is that a work-week is roughly 36 hours of actual working time, net of mandatory meetings and break-time. Using this math, 150 person-hours is roughly the equivalent of one person-month.

Second, from a prioritization point of view, statutory and regulatory initiatives get the highest priority. I have allocated resources first to these initiatives.

Third, transactional (pyramid layer 2) initiatives can be contentious. Even though I feel that they are context in most organizations and not core, the level of investment can sometimes be high, meriting this for inclusion on the portfolio management grid. Think of an ERP release-level upgrade, for example. I have concluded that including this layer should be a case-by-case consideration.

When working at the division level, I have included initiatives driven by headquarters in this same bucket. In such cases, I have had to keep my division business heads informed of the diversion to help attain a corporate goal.

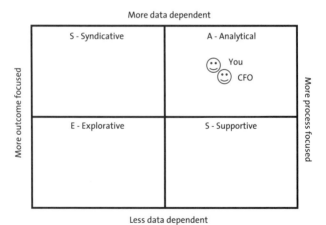

Figure 6.1 - Step 2 - Meshing your world-view with the CFO

Finally, once I have made these assumptions about Portfolio Planning, I have used a 2 x 2 grid to plot my plans. On the horizontal (X) axis, I like to plot investments in absolute dollars, regardless of the period of time over which the investment is made. On the vertical (Y) axis, I like to plot the expected ROI.

It is important here to make sure that the methods used to calculate both Investment and ROI are consistent across all entries on the grid. Whatever method is chosen should also be held true to form for an extended period of time (in my case, at least 4 quarters). The same person, or group of people, should preferably use the same set of tools and approaches to consistently calculate these variables. That way, biases are equivalently captured, reflected, and cancelled out.

You will notice that there are no specific graduations on either the X-axis or the Y-axis. And this is deliberately so. Depending on the business climate, an enterprise can set the "cut-off" lines where it makes most sense. Sharing this with the CFO in a discussion to set these lines is a good way to syndicate opinion among the C-level staff. At the end of the day, a tool like this helps the enterprise determine where to place focus. And that is the essence of good decision-making, especially when demand far exceeds supply as it usually does with IT organizations.

Relevance of this matrix to the CIO and CFO discussion

There are two reasons that this Portfolio Planning grid should be an item on the agenda. Firstly, all new initiatives that meet the minimum threshold and are accepted into the queue should have been subjected to the Investment and ROI calculations that place it in one of the four appropriate quadrants.

The second, significantly more important, reason is to ensure that both the Investment and the ROI are appropriately measured and reported to create full transparency. And this should be a joint effort between the CIO and CFO organizations.

While many, if not most, businesses have an adequate methodology to measure the total investment in a given initiative, I know of only a few businesses that have the rigor to revisit the initiatives and measure the return on investment. This is an area that is best tackled by the CFO organization. As IT investments are no different from any other investments made for the general benefit of the business, foregoing such an examination robs the business of an opportunity to learn from real-life experiments being initiated within itself for its own benefit!

It is surprising how few organizations have put such a discipline in place. Fewer still exercise the discipline rigorously, and deliver feedback to the larger organization.

Other financial metrics in CFO and CIO discussions

Between the three metrics of CapEx, OpEx and cost-per-unit-of-delivery, the health and strength of the CIO organization can be ascertained. Of course, all three should have budgets, goals and targets to begin with. The discussions between the CIO and CFO should track absolute variances that exceed more than 5 percent, in my opinion.

The Insightful CIO continually reviews these three measures with the CFO. Forecasts may change with time. The idea is not only to be on target, but to continually ensure both understanding and alignment in all three.

Business leaders set different thresholds to consider and classify an outlay of cash to be either CapEx or OpEx. The CFO and CIO should both be on the same page regarding these thresholds. Changes in law and business conditions sometimes prompt changes in the threshold for CapEx and OpEx. The impact of such changes on the IT portfolio should be jointly examined by the CFO and CIO.

The Insightful CIO clearly understands the impact of IT initiatives on the Balance Sheet and the P&L. She understands that CapEx intensive projects deplete the cash-reserves of the business. She also clearly understands how depreciation and amortization impact the P&L statement. She understands when to expense an initiative versus when to treat an initiative as a capitalization opportunity. It is also worth noting that business policies governing spending can mean different things to different people. I often find this in the use of the term "Labor dollars" on a budget. CFOs typically translate this into equivalent heads—also called FTE, or Full-Time Equivalents—and implicitly hold the CIO accountable to the FTE number.

However, in this age of global talent availability, the real cost per FTE may not be globally applicable. In fact, especially in information technology, where talent outsourcing—particularly from regions of the world that present a labor-cost arbitrage opportunity without compromising quality, like India—is almost de rigeur, a CFO and CIO are better off agreeing to a total dollar spending number, rather than an FTE number. Using this approach, the CIO will have much better flexibility in mixing on-shore FTEs and off-shore resources and managing the mix in a fashion that best suits the needs of the business.

As senior executives of the business, the CIO and CFO should discuss how to deal with all the IT initiatives in the pipeline effectively, in light of the current financial status of the business. If a specific initiative has—or group of interrelated initiatives have—the potential to impact the financial health of the business adversely, the CFO and CIO have the duty of care to inform the beneficiary in the business appropriately. Perhaps the initiative can be done sooner, deferred until a better time, differently funded, or even cancelled and be reassessed at a later time.

Cost-per-unit of Delivery

In a previous chapter, where we developed the framework of the pyramid and the extensions to it, I suggested that the first two layers of the pyramid—Infrastructure and Transactional layers—should both be viewed as contextual to providing the business with basic, transactional information systems. I also suggested that Quality Assurance—not just software quality assurance but overall information technology-wide Quality Assurance should be viewed as context activity, and not core.

Each of these is a candidate for measurement using the cost-per-unit-of-delivery method. While it is easy to leave the reader with this thought, it is quite difficult to design and develop metrics that accurately reflect the CIO organization capabilities using this approach, without subverting the motivation and losing sight of the objective.

Any change or innovation in approach should directly support a lower spending. However, the path to lower spending may not be without hurdles. With infrastructure, it is often difficult to lower the spending unless there is an up-front investment in improved infrastructure, and so on. I personally prefer and recommend using IRR to justify investments in IT infrastructure.

These are topics of interest to both the CFO and the CIO. By enlisting the help of CFOs and their organizations, CIO organizations stand a much better chance to design and develop a set of metrics that appropriately capture and measure the total cost of solution delivery than doing it on their own. This approach has two up-sides:

1 CFO organizations do this as a part of their charter

2 It demonstrates to the organization as a whole

that the IT function is willing to be held to clear, consistent and transparent accountability.

Core? Or Context?

To set the context, I outline a history of accounting practices. In 1934, the Securities and Exchange Commission (SEC) was set up as the federal statutory body with the authority to establish standards for financial accounting and reporting for publicly traded companies. Over the years, the SEC has developed guidelines. It has relied on non-Governmental institutions to create many standards.

Following the Security Exchange Act of 1934, the American Institute of Certified Public Accountants (AICPA) stepped up to develop the Generally Accepted Accounting Practices, or GAAP, in short. The AICPA created a sub-body—the Accounting Principles Board (APB) to focus on GAAP in 1959.

In 1973, the APB was replaced with an independent, not-for-profit board called the Financial Accounting Standards Board, or FASB, for short. FASB's mission is "to establish and improve standards of financial accounting and reporting for the guidance and education of the public, including issuers, auditors, and users of financial information."

FASB is U.S.-centric. So were the FASB's predecessor organizations. With increasing and accelerating globalization, there has been an emerging need for an international body with a similar focus—a global standard that enables businesses to be measured equivalently, regardless of their country of origin or operation.

In 2001, the International Accounting Standards Board, or IASB, was formally launched. The IASB is committed to developing a single set of high quality, understandable, and globally enforceable accounting standards that require transparent and comparable information in general purpose financial statements. In addition, the IASB co-operates with the different national accounting standards bodies to achieve convergence in accounting standards around the world.

Given this rich pedigree, a large body of Accounting principles and standards has emerged. While this body of standards continues to evolve, the original GAAP standards governing the day-to-day operations of a business "as usual" have been around for decades.

Standards governing "extraordinary" events continue to evolve—a reflection of the various exotic and quirky business transactions entered into and conducted by businesses, as they engage in new business methods in an increasingly flat world.

When business proceeds "as usual" in the normal course of operations, the Finance organization acts as a score-keeper to the game of business—providing a yardstick to measure and judge business performance.

However, every so often in business, events that are not "business as usual" occur. Law suits are settled. Mergers, acquisitions and divestitures change the constitution and identity of the business. Joint venture agreements and strategic investments change the business landscape. Non-core assets, like land and buildings, are traded. Companies go public or de-list from bourses to "go private." Such "extraordinary" events tend to be strategic in nature. These events are usually discussed at the Board level before companies commit to a specific course of action. Depending on circumstance, Finance moves from being context to core during such a phase in the business. The Insightful CIO has an agenda item that specifically calls out the phase of the business. If the business is in the middle of an extraordinary event, he engages in a discussion to understand the accounting and finance nuances; and ensures that the needful IT support mechanisms are in place to appropriately record and report such events.

Summary

CFOs and CIOs actually have a lot in common. They are both heads of what are traditionally labeled General and Administrative (G&A) functions. They both have a charter to provide a vital "context" to the business by reducing the friction of doing business and creating clear visibility. An organization that boasts of a great CIO will likely have an equivalently good CFO.

The Insightful CIO recognizes these shared attributes. He proceeds to focus on and create this special gestalt with the CFO, so as to leverage their combined strengths for the benefit of the business.

Agenda for discussion with the CFO

A first-time agenda - Developing a relationship
1. Conversation with CEO - Strategy alignment
2. Conversations with other C-level executives - Level-set
3. Self-discovery: Your plot-point on the ASsESs frame
4. Validation: Your plot-point from the CFO's POV
5. Hypothesis: Your POV of plot-point
6. Co-Discovery: Their plot-point on the same frame
7. Establish context - The pyramid with a backdrop
8. General feedback regarding the CIO organization

Agenda for recurring conversations:
1. Balance Sheet, P&L, Planning and Budgeting tools
2. Statutory and regulatory compliance (SOX, PCI etc)
3. Framework to measure IT value-initiatives and IT cost-per-unit utilities
4. Portfolio review framework/ROI/Success metrics
5. CIO sponsored activities
6. IT Financials
7. Extraordinary business events: Adequacy of IT support

8. Emerging standards and tools - An open discussion
9. Any feedback for the CIO organization?

Insights and probes

1. The CFO organization is heavily relied upon by the CEO and the Board to accurately reflect the health of the business. The Board typically charters Audits, to be sure that the health of the business is independently validated. Do you understand the charter and concerns of the CFO organization?

2. The CFO tends to be a busy executive, especially around period-ends (like month-ends, quarter-ends etc). How often do you and the CFO meet on a one-on-one basis? Are these regularly scheduled meetings? Face to face? Do such meetings get cancelled? Often? Why?

3. CFOs are usually privy to possible future events, since their organization is tapped by the CEO to project the financial implications of such events. What are some of the regular topics of conversation between the two of you?

4. CFO organizations can help in creating transparent reporting mechanisms. Does your CEO feel that you are doing a good job in transparently reflecting your activities in investments and spending?

5. CFOs can serve as a useful bridge, and as a trusted ally, in communicating how IT monies are invested for the benefit of the business. Have you leveraged your CFO organization in this fashion? Do the business unit heads feel that they have transparent visibility into IT activities? Do they understand how their money gets invested in IT enablement? Do they concur that they are getting value for their investments? How do they provide you and your team with feedback?

6. Businesses regularly trade-off investment choices, using some means to assess all the options on hand at any given time. Most often, this tends to be a Portfolio Assessment tool of some sort. Do you have a Portfolio management framework? If so, do you and your colleagues agree that the right priorities are continually addressed?

7. CFOs can occasionally become focused on headcount, rather than spending. Does your business manage

labor costs based on budget dollars? Or is it based on FTE numbers?

8. Infrastructure and transaction-processing are KTLO ("keep the lights on") items; and deserve to be measured on a cost-per-unit-of-delivery basis. Do you have a suite of cost-per-unit-of-delivery metrics at the lower two layers of the pyramid? What about the cost per unit of quality? How often is it tracked? How often is it reported? To whom is it reported?

Mental modeling for the neophyte

1. How well do you understand the charter of the CFO organization? Do you have a "buddy" in that organization? How often do you and your buddy get together? Do you discuss IT financials when you do?

2. If you do not have a background in reading, interpreting and understanding financial statements, have you considered enrolling in such courses as "Finance for Non-Financial Executives"? Many educational institutions offer such courses.

3. Do you know your cost per FTE on-shore? Do you

have access to off-shore resources? What are their FTE costs?

4. Do you understand how to help your business colleagues deal with shortage of resources? Money? Additional people?

5. How well do you understand the layers in the pyramid? Do you have an explicit understanding of the elemental costs in each layer? Or do you just react when the going gets squeezed?

6. Do you philosophically agree that infrastructure and transactional services should be measured on a cost-per-unit-of-delivery method? If you do not, what is your philosophy? If you do, do you understand how best to engage with the CFO organization to develop such a set of metrics?

7. Hail The Rain Maker

From "The COO—An Enigma to Many"

Mario Morino, The Chairman's Corner,
May 2006

- **The Executor.** One role of the COO is to lead the execution of strategies developed by top management. It is simply a concession to the complexity and scope of the CEO's job today, with its numerous external constituents. The COO takes responsibility for delivering results on a day-to-day basis, while the CEO is focused on the strategic, long-term challenges and major opportunities.

- **The Change Agent.** Sometimes the COO is used to lead a specific strategic initiative, such as a turnaround, a major organizational change, or a planned rapid expansion. This requires the COO to have a degree of unquestioned authority similar to that of an executor COO.

- **The Mentor.** Some organizations use a COO to mentor a young or inexperienced CEO (often a founder). A rapidly growing entrepreneurial venture might seek an industry veteran with seasoning, wisdom, and a rich network who can develop both the CEO and the emerging business.

- **The Other Half.** A role that complements the CEO's experience, style, knowledge base, or penchants. For instance, providing a "calm, self-effacing manner."

- **The Partner.** Sometimes a CEO simply works better with a partner, a form of co-leadership management.

- **The Heir Apparent.** Sometimes the role of a COO is to groom—or test—a business' CEO-elect, and gives the person a chance to learn the whole business, its business, environment, and people. Being identified as a likely heir to the role of CEO is not a guarantee.

- **The MVP.** Some companies offer the job of COO as a promotion to an executive considered too valuable to lose.

Ashwin Rangan

The Man. The Go-to guy. Mr. Get-It-Done. Mr. Fix It. I have heard these, and many other such titles to describe the Chief Operating Officer (COO).

The COO is an organization's back-stop to the senior management team. Great COOs bring grace under pressure to the senior management team. They take the mundane and make it seem elegant. Great COOs are jacks of many trades and, maybe, master of one. They define themselves more by who they are than by what they do. Their bailiwick can be wide, and their style is usually both winsome and influencing. They are neither the Engineer nor the Driver; but they "keep the trains running on time". Their information needs can vary, depending on the crisis-du-jour.

The Insightful CIO understands these parameters well. She develops a good working relationship with the COO, who usually has a good read on the pulse of the organization.

Regardless of what may be suggested by the title of COO, CIOs should be careful in considering and addressing requests for technology enablement when it comes from the COO or from his office. Given the time-constant to develop and deliver an appropriate

IT solution, the CIO should first carefully assess the significance and time-value of the request before committing resources.

It is worth noting that COOs are usually "get it done" guys. As such, quick-and-dirty IT solutions that help them solve their problem of the day are quite acceptable to COOs.

The COO's world

Not all businesses have a COO—a reason the role remains an enigma to many people; and to many companies. Many organizations may combine this role into that of a CEO. Needless to say that the CEO in such an organization can be under considerable pressure. This is because, as CEO, he has to fulfill the—usually—externally-facing obligations of the organization; and as COO, he has to fulfill the—usually—internally-focused day-to-day initiatives of the organization.

When a business has a COO in fact, it is usually a special individual who figures out how best to be effective in this role. Rare is the case of a COO who is effective and enjoys this role —a role that is "neither fish nor fowl." And even rarer is the case that successful COOs remain in the role of a COO for an extended period of many years. This has made me question what makes a successful COO, many times, and I find many answers.

The Parable of the Hedgehog and the Fox

Archilochus, a poet-philosopher in ancient Greece, first documented the difference between the hedgehog and the fox. He pithily stated, "The Fox knows many things, but the Hedgehog knows one big thing." In 1953, Sir Isaiah Berlin, one of the leading Western political philosophers and liberal thinkers of the 20th century, expanded on and expounded the differences between these character types. In a now-legendary monograph, he chose to use this ancient parable to characterize world-views.

In summary, Berlin categorizes his subjects—writers and thinkers who were his contemporaries, mostly—as Foxes or Hedgehogs. The idea is that foxes view the world through a variety of lenses that are their experiences, while hedgehogs view the world through a single filter. I invite the reader to research this monograph available online. The distinction between the Fox and the Hedgehog is no doubt artificial and polarized. Nonetheless, it reveals a fundamental difference in world-view that invites both inspection and introspection.

In my experience, great COOs have been more fox than hedgehog, and from this I have now concluded that truly remarkable COOs share several traits: they know many things; they are comfortable dealing with simultaneously divergent objectives; they are able to resolve complex issues quickly and boil them to a few clear priorities; they are passionate to know and to continuously learn from a variety of sources and experiences; they develop many abilities without becoming fixated with any single point of view; they are able to see the world from many different perspectives. If I had to pick on a single word in the English language to capture their virtue, it would be "simultaneous."

The role of the COO

It is rare for the COO to have a large staff. Such an organization is more an exception rather than the rule. Many times, COOs are a staff function to the CEO, with a few key direct reports. On rare occasion, COOs have a handful of senior level executives reporting to them, who, in turn, have organizations that report to them. The COO's responsibility and charter can vary, depending on the specific combination of the needs of the business and the comfort level of the CEO.

I have found some very typical characteristics that define a COO's responsibilities within the enterprise. The COO is an internally-focused senior executive. His primary charter is to ensure that the customer value-creation and delivery chain is free of friction. A secondary charter is to enable flawless execution once the business' strategic alternatives are considered and decisions have been made. A third is an observation. Great COOs seem very comfortable doing whatever it takes to make the every-day modalities seem elegant. They architect and make accountable an organization that eventually prides itself on keeping trains running on time.

In this, the COO is like a CEO. He has a small staff, but large responsibilities. The difference is that the COO has his hand on the day-to-day pulse of the business focused internally, while the CEO has his hand on the strategic pulse of the business, with an external market focus.

A great team of a CEO paired with a COO is a sort of yin-yang relationship, with each being perfectly complementary of the other. Both of them use a combination of the inherent power of organizational chain-of-command and inter-personal influence to get teams motivated and directed towards common goals. American business has had many storied 2-man teams, operating as CEO and COO. I am sure that you know of one such team, if not more. Perhaps you work in one such organization that is blessed to have a "dynamic duo," guiding the course of your organization.

A hypothesis of the COO's world-view

I recall here for the reader's benefit the ASsESs framework from a few chapters back. In that, we created a 2 X 2 matrix to reflect the way in which world-views can be categorized.

COOs are a natural in the quadrant that was labeled Syndicator—she is the executive who is held accountable by the CEO in ensuring that all bases are covered, especially in the domain of business execution.

Thus, COOs will typically look first for data to support implementing decisions. As typical "syndicators," they will quickly enumerate every functional area impacted, and use this information to influence each of the stake-holders to lend their support in successfully implementing the decision. Finally, they will syndicate the collective, ensuring that there are no unattended dependencies in execution.

Great COOs are like military Generals who are at the front-line. They make complex "military manoeuvres" seem easy and graceful. Such is their impact on the business! The key to understanding typical COO behavior is that they have an inherent urgency and a bias towards execution.

Developing a shared vision with the COO

Given their charter and natural bias, it may be tempting to conclude that COOs do not have a long-term and relatively more strategic perspective on initiatives. Such a conclusion would be incorrect. Great COOs have a terrific sense of what it takes to implement the long-term strategies that the business has chosen. Compared to an externally-facing CEO, the COO has a sense for the inter-functional dynamics and dependencies in implementing such a strategy. They are better clued-in about the competing priorities for resources. Extending the analogy of "keeping the trains running on time," while the CEO knows that there trains in the business and that they are on track and running, the COO knows the specific location and speed of all the trains running within the business.

Thus they are able to make quick and insightful implementation decisions that minimize the possibility of train collisions. Part of their role is to retain this world-view of the entire train system in mind, while making decisions pertaining to the specific "train-of-the-moment."

The Insightful CIO forges a strong working relationship with the COO, and leveraging such a relationship, he gets a good "read" on the pulse of the organization. The advantage of such a relationship is that the CIO can get a 360-view of the business from a single whistle-stop!

To engender this relationship, the Insightful CIO engages the COO in a wide-ranging dialogue, creating a fluid and fruitful agenda that spans every functional area within the business, not necessarily with the same intensity. Leading agenda topics should focus on the core value-discipline of the business, depending on the nature of the business. However, given the nature of information technology and the ability of the CIO organization to positively impact outcomes, a good share of time and thought should also be invested in context.

A great COO-CIO relationship typically helps businesses tease apart and address both core and context initiatives. COOs can help CIOs to appropriately vector scarce IT resources to do appropriate justice to both. COOs can assist CIOs to connect better with the right functional linkage-points at the right time, in order to maximize the probability of success in the core areas of the business. In the areas that are context to the business, COOs can champion initiatives to lower the total cost of doing business.

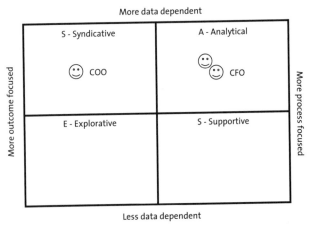

Figure 7.1 - Step 3 - Gestalt with the COO's POV added-in

Ashwin Rangan

Elements of a dialog between the COO and the CIO

As we have already discussed, COOs are pragmatists. Thus their interest in theories and frameworks is heightened if such tools help them to get to a finish-line faster. Not for them the elegance of a theory that resolves a complex theoretical problem!

Risk management and compliance

Statutory and regulatory compliance is a part of the cost of doing business. To comply with the industry-specific requirements, subject matter experts (SME) in specific areas often drive the compliance initiative. For example, the Chief Investment Officer in a bank is most likely the senior executive shepherding a Basel II initiative.

"So what's the point?" you might ask. The point is that while the SME—by virtue of being an expert—is likely to expound on the elegance of the Basel II framework, the COO, being the pragmatic fox is not always interested in the inherent beauty of a compliance framework. He is interested in getting things done. The Insightful CIO recognizes the power of having such a strong and pragmatic implementation partner. He builds and leverages a good relationship with the COO, co-opting the COO into supporting the more contentious initiatives, and pushes such initiatives across the finish-line.

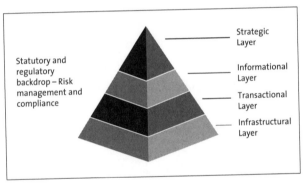

Figure 7.2 - The IT Pyramid with the zones of interest to the COO shown shaded

Ashwin Rangan

Transaction processing

The ownership of the ERP—or Enterprise Resource Planning —systems has been a big issue in many businesses. ERP systems have so many modules that they touch most functional areas in a typical organization.

Vendors targeting smaller businesses have sold ERP as sophisticated financial accounting systems—and not surprisingly—to the CFO organizations. In larger, more complex businesses, ERP system implementations have been sold as business transformative tools. For years now, salespeople have targeted the CEO. In large-cap organizations, since about the mid-1990s, the decision to undertake an ERP implementation has often been an item on the Board Room agenda. Directors started to read and better understand the level of effort, costs and risks associated with such business-transformative ERP implementations. Instances of failed implementation became legendary towards the middle of the 1990s, adding a touch of panic to such discussions. Given the broad-based nature of ERP packages, its influence can touch many different functional specialties in the business—from Sales at the front of the business to Human Resources at the very back of the business.

Recalling the 4-layer pyramid framework, ERP is clearly in the second layer up, just above the infrastructure layer. It is the heart of the transaction layer in the IT pyramid of a business. This is the layer that captures and ensures the timeliness, completeness and integrity of all data. This lays the foundation for decision-making downstream.

It is not unusual for the CEO of the business to champion the effort during the up-front implementation of ERP. Such a sponsorship is only right, given the attendant Board Room visibility. ERP implementations have the potential to disrupt businesses, in the course of implementation, or at the time of transition from the old environment to the new, integrated ERP environment. If the ERP implementation is in support of a business transformative initiative, it will need the sponsorship of the CEO in order to have an improved chance of success.

However, when the ERP becomes operational, CEOs typically move on to championing other strategic initiatives. Often, the ERP system is orphaned at this stage. All too often, CIOs have to carry the burden of justifying and defending subsequent ERP-centric decisions. They become the de-facto sponsors of resource-consuming ERP efforts, like upgrades, or web-enabling the ERP system. The problem here is that CIOs are only providers, not consumers, of ERP systems and services, regardless of their own capabilities and self-perceptions. This clearly leads to a misalignment of accountabilities.

The COO is a natural to take over ownership of this layer of the pyramid. Given his charter as the Syndicator in the business, he is ideally positioned to champion broad-based, inter-functional initiatives. He is much better positioned than the CIO to determine whether and when to undertake complex initiatives that have the potential to simultaneously disrupt multiple functional areas; and to weigh the benefits vis-à-vis the risks and the outcomes. In this, he is the business's best candidate to own the ERP environment.

Possibly strategic, but unproven technologies

In a related but different vein, given their practical, get-it-done bias, COOs can be great business partners for CIO organizations to test and pilot quick-and-dirty technologies and approaches. An example may illustrate this point.

It is quite common for a small, innovative software business to create differentiated capabilities that could be of benefit to businesses. Good recent examples are Wikis and Blogs.

CIO organizations can see the benefit of Wikis, but it is still early days to find a stable corporate sponsor who will carry this capability into the organization, exploring its potential and leveraging the benefits. As with any new innovative capability, it is not yet clear how best to mainstream Wikis. It has yet to cross the chasm, to use a Geoffrey Moore term, within most businesses.

CIO organizations today have this wonderful opportunity to discuss the potential of this emerging tool with the COO, explain the ease with which a Wiki environment can be set-up, and engage in a broad dialog with the COO about possible areas of application. An

Ashwin Rangan

example may be in creating a self-help Wiki environment facing the customer. Such an environment could lead to the creation of a powerful feedback mechanism for the business on the one side, and an equally powerful self-help, community-driven, UGC (User Generated Content) rich learning tool, on the other side. These activities could help in maintaining flat or reducing the cost-per-unit-of-delivery of widgets to customers.

Such a topic is not the exclusive preserve of any one functional area of the business. Inputs to such a discussion are typically unstructured. Since many functional areas may be impacted, such an initiative is unlikely to find a single natural champion for sponsorship.

Given this background, the COO can serve as a powerful sponsor for a highly-visible initiative that pilots a new technology. Given his vantage point, the COO can help the CIO organization to point Wikis at the right problem-spaces, and maximize the business benefit. An early "win" with such a new technology will help it find the sea-legs that it needs in order to spread out into other possible areas of applicability within the business.

A fellow-steward at the prioritization table

Perhaps the most valuable partnership between the CIO and the COO is seen when IT faces its oldest business conundrum: finite IT resources having to meet infinite business demands. CIOs typically create some forum or the other to resolve such a contention-in the most sophisticated instances, they create an IT Steering Council that works with the numerous departments requesting IT help. In smaller IT shops, it may just be a list of requests created by the CIO and his team.

Regardless of the specific nature of the forum, the CIO will likely find the COO to have a sympathetic ear. While the CIO may only face such a bake-off once every so often, the COO is a daily-adept at such bake-offs. The Insightful CIO enlists the COO's active participation and seeks his help to resolve this conundrum.

An added benefit to this approach is that the COO now becomes a part-owner of the priorities that are assigned. He is now a more aware senior executive colleague. By virtue of his daily vantage-point, the COO is in a position to mobilize the organization's resources appropriately to support IT initiatives.

We talked about how the CFO could help CIOs with portfolio rationalization and management previously. In businesses that have a COO, the troika of COO, CFO and CIO is ideal to make 360-Decisions. They would bring a pragmatic view of the probable, a financial view of the prudent and a technical view of the possible to the table respectively. A well-informed CEO will immediately see this as his best change-management council; and both anoint and promote it as such.

A win-win-win for the entire business.

The Core versus Context

Great COOs improve the context to a business. They create, validate, facilitate, synergize and catalyze the medium in which the business thrives. While they can fight fires everyday, they can operate equally well in the stratosphere of strategy. In all of this, they are very much the core. This said, it is common to find the COO in well-run businesses become sponsor of extraordinary initiatives: the steward of post-merger integration, a leader with responsibility for quietly determining the strategy and steps to a proposed lay-off, the C-level executive who is working closely with an external agency on a rebranding initiative.

Size and complexity are often driver-variables in determining whether an organization has a COO or not. If the organization is small or simple, a CEO may be able to wear both the CEO and the COO hats effectively. If such is the case, the CEO takes on the responsibilities that are attached to the COO in this chapter.

Summary

Great COOs are irreplaceable. They are more mortar than brick. They are more music than the words in a song. They orchestrate the day-to-day activities of the enterprise.

The Insightful CIO forges a strong relationship with an effective COO. A wonderful 3-way relationship between the COO, the CFO and the CIO could serve a business as one of the strongest general management teams in the enterprise.

Agenda for discussion with the COO
A first-time agenda - Developing a relationship

1. Conversation with CEO - Strategy alignment
2. Conversations with other C-level executives - Level-set
3. Self-discovery: Your plot-point on the ASsESs frame
4. Validation: Your plot-point from his POV
5. Hypothesis: Your POV of his plot-point
6. Co-Discovery: His plot-point on the same frame
7. Establish context—The pyramid with a backdrop
8. General feedback regarding the CIO organization

A repeating agenda - Leveraging the relationship

1. General initiatives review
2. Risk management and compliance
3. Broadbased IT initiatives like ERP
4. IT initiatives - Friction points; Greasing required
5. Assessment of the enterprise's overall stamina and morale for change
6. Portfolio prioritization
7. Emerging standards and tools—An open discussion
8. Feedback for the CIO organization

Insights and probes

1. Not all businesses have a Chief Operating Officer. Even when there is one, different COOs have different accountabilities. Does your business have a COO? Or a senior executive chartered with the accountabilities of a COO? How well do you understand his accountabilities? How well do you relate to the COO?

2. Take a moment to reflect about your business's COO. In which ASsESs quadrant does your COO naturally operate?

3. As busy executives, CxOs have their days filled with meetings. How often do you and the COO meet? What is on your discussion agenda?

4. All businesses have a core and a context. Good businesses become great as they continue to enhance the core over time. To paraphrase Jack Welch, they continuously look to "take their back office and make it into someone else's front office." Is there clear differentiation between Core and Context in your business? How did the leadership team approach this discussion?

5. Whether or not you have a commercial off-the-shelf package for transaction processing, your business has a transaction-intensive ERP layer. Who owns the ERP environment in your business?

6. Typically, COOs focus on a wide range of interesting initiatives. Some are in the core of the business. Many are not. Oftentimes, these initiatives which are not core to the business offer an opportunity to try out new technologies and approaches. Have you recently piloted any new technologies or approaches with your COO? For what initiative?

Mental modeling for the neophyte

1. Knowing the COO of your business is a good idea. Do you know who it is? More interestingly, does she know who you are? Have you had a chance to meet with her? If not, chart out an agenda and meet with her at the earliest opportunity. Get to know her accountabilities.

2. Reflect on your business. What is the discipline at which it excels? This will likely be the core of the business. How well do you relate to the core of the business?

Who is chartered with the day-to-day running of the core of the business? Do you know them? Get to know them well. Meet with them regularly so that you can learn more about the core.

3. Think about the transactional environment wherein data is typically captured and processed, day in and day out. Is this a holistic, homogenous transaction processing environment? Does data flow smoothly and easily, as water in an unobstructed river? Or is the flow interrupted, as dams would obstruct the flow of water in a river? How can you enable an uninterrupted, yet well monitored and regulated, flow?

4. I am sure you get a lot of mail from vendors who would love to get an opportunity to pitch their products to you. How often have you invited them to do so? Have any of their offerings looked promising? To solve some business problem? Perhaps not entirely, but at least most of the way? Perhaps you can engage your COO in a dialog to bring in such a capability on a pilot basis.

Section 3: Bonding With The Best

"Some are born great, some achieve greatness, and some hire public relations officers."

Daniel J. Boorstin
US Librarian of Congress, 1975 to 1987;
American historian, professor, attorney and writer

I am sure that you have interacted with CIOs in course of your career. Some of them have been good. A few have been great. And you have asked yourself the same question as have I, "What makes these folks great? How did they become so insightful?"

One thing I have noticed is that CEOs do not hesitate to put great CIOs in front of their Boards. Another is that great CIOs seem to have some attributes in common with one another. In the following chapters, I would like to explore these two topics in greater detail.

8. Shooting Birdies In The Boardroom

"Every company, every boardroom in which I sit, has a plan, and they have objectives, goals, and a process. And to make it work, the pressure and incentive have to come from the top."

Vernon Jordan
Member of the Board of some of the
best-known Brands in the world

IT Governance is a process that is held as a joint custody by the board of directors and the management team of an organization. It is also one of the least well-understood facets of IT—by the CIO, by the senior management teams in enterprises and, sadly, by directors on boards. IT Governance is all about how these custodians deal with understanding, directing, supervising, monitoring and controlling IT activities in their organization.

IT Governance is becoming increasingly critical to organizations in a networked economy. In businesses that are primarily about IT—like Ebay, Google or Yahoo!, for example—IT governance is paramount for obvious reasons. Interestingly, another genre of businesses rely so heavily upon IT that one could argue that IT is their business. Good examples are e-Tailers, like walmart.com and Amazon, and financial institutions like Bank of America and Citibank. In such businesses, IT governance is clearly very important.

More interestingly, traditional businesses have come to rely heavily upon IT to compete better and to sustain competitive advantage. In fact, in recent years, over 50 percent of the capital spending in the US economy is on IT in aggregate and IT-related items. Of course, the intensity of such spending varies from one industry vertical to the next; and from one business to the next within the same vertical.

Nonetheless, the point remains that IT continues to be an increasingly larger fraction of capital spending in the US economy. The need to be sure that these investments are returning commensurate returns has never been greater. Yet, IT governance continues to lag as a topic of rigorous discussion in the boardroom. One of the contributing factors is that directors tend to be non-technical.

The Board Room and Directors: What are their duties?

There are many sources of reference regarding Board Room duties and responsibilities available on the Internet. Since there is a multiplicity of material available, there is no "one reference" that serves as a gold-standard, so to speak, for Board Room duties. There are many—and sometimes, conflicting—points of view. The following is a set of roles suggested in Brenda Hanlon's In Boards We Trust. According to this book, Boards:

1. Provide continuity for the organization by setting up a corporation or legal existence, and to represent the organization's point of view through interpretation of its products and services, and advocacy for them

2. Select and appoint a chief executive to whom responsibility for the administration of the organization is delegated, including:

- to review and evaluate his/her performance regularly on the basis of a specific job description, including executive relations with the board, leadership in the organization, in program planning and implementation, and in management of the organization and its personnel

- to offer administrative guidance and determine whether to retain or dismiss the executive

3. Govern the organization through policies and objectives, formulated and agreed upon by the chief executive and employees, and assigning priorities and ensure the organization's capacity to carry out programs through continuous reviews

4. Acquire sufficient resources for the organization's operations and to finance the products and services adequately

5. Account to the public for the products and services of the organization and expenditures of its funds, including:

- to provide for fiscal accountability, approve the budget, and formulate policies related to contracts from public or private resources

- to accept responsibility for all conditions and policies attached to new, innovative, or experimental programs.

In other words, Boards are expected to set business strategy, understand and manage risks, measure business performance and deliver value to shareowners. These expectations can only be realized if the governance frameworks are both appropriate and adequate—whether it is for IT or any other function.

IT governance in the Board Room

IT governance is not substantially different from any other form of governance. The only difference is that IT involves an understanding of information technology. In this sense, it is no different from any other area of governance that brings with it a need for in-depth understanding of that specific subject area. The purpose of IT governance is to direct IT activities from the board room. Appropriate governance ensures multiple objectives:

- To align IT with the enterprise in order to realize the benefits of IT investments
- To exploit market opportunities and maximize benefits by leveraging IT assets

- To use IT resources in a responsible manner
- To understand, manage and mitigate IT-induced risks to the enterprise

The first step in IT governance is to set objectives. This sets the direction, the "tone at the top." The next step is for IT to develop a set of initiatives that are in alignment with the business objectives. The goal of such activities should be to define, develop and deploy capabilities that impact the efficiency of the organization positively, thereby driving economic benefits in service of the shareowners. The third step in IT governance is to measure the effectiveness of IT initiatives. The goal of this step is manifold. If the IT initiative being measured is focused on improving an aspect of business that is already automated, the goal should be to measure the ins and outs and compare them with other industry benchmarks. If, on the other hand, the IT initiative being measured is focused on creating a newly automated environment, the goal should be to measure the quantum change in productivity. The last step in IT governance is to provide a holistic view of IT-induced risks (such as IT security, IT readiness in case of business discontinuity, IT's role in meeting statutory and regulatory compliance requirements) to the board. The following figure captures the framework:

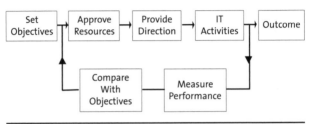

Figure 8.1 - A closed-loop approach to IT governance in the board room

Why is IT governance important?

As IT spending continues to increase, IT governance continues to gain in importance. But besides this obvious reason, there are numerous other reasons to emphasize IT governance.

IT is regarded as one of the highest leverage points in creating shareowner value in the 21st century. IT is

Ashwin Rangan

already critical to automating and recording the results from a variety of day-to-day activities, like Accounting and Finance, Production and Operations Management, Supply Chain Planning and Management, Sales and Marketing. IT is increasingly important as a source of enterprise transformation, leading to the development and delivery of new products and services to an established customer base. A significantly large number of businesses are investing in and experimenting with IT capabilities across their global facilities. Innovation today drives the development and the delivery of new products and services in a decentralized and globally dispersed fashion. Think contract manufacturing in China, contract customer-care facilities in India and contract global logistics operators, like DHL and FedEx, who operate as the glue to pull it all together and hold it.

Despite such tectonic shifts in business practices directly resulting from new capabilities underpinned by IT and involving high risk and large investments, IT is typically not reviewed with the same intensity by Boards as, for instance, are company finances and new product development.

There are many underlying reasons for this.

On the one hand, Boards tend to be composed of

directors from the investment, financial and general business communities. Each of these tends to have an excellent understanding of business, in general; but not necessarily of IT, in particular.

On the other hand, IT is a relatively young discipline. It is only in the last 50 years that this "discipline" has come into being. On a timescale measuring business activity in general, 50 years is just a blip. So much so that formal rules for IT governance are still evolving.

IT started out by simply being a faster adding machine. With developments in communications protocols and networking, it has quickly grown very complex. Added to this, the rate of change in IT continues to increase, making it difficult even for IT professionals to keep abreast of new developments and capabilities.

As the enterprise has expanded to include extended global supply chains, the boundaries of the enterprise have been redrawn, using IT as the tool to do so. In the global networked economy, IT is now one of the most complex twines that hold together the enterprise. And not the least, IT has been treated as an entity that is separate from the business—rather like a tool-maker in a manufacturing plant.

Ashwin Rangan

This analogy was perhaps adequate when IT was just a simple but faster adding machine. Given today's realities, the analogy is no longer applicable. Combining all of these factors, appropriate and adequate IT governance is critical to the continued success of an enterprise, especially now. IT is now an integral and pervasive element of business in almost all enterprises.

Expectation vs. reality: The (mis)match in the board room

While the case for IT governance is clear, there is a mismatch between expectations and reality.

Corporate Boards expect the organization's management to fulfill certain basics while leveraging IT. These basics are explained below.

Boards would like to ensure that IT is aligned with the business. Boards expect the CIO function to

deliver high quality IT solutions—on time, on budget, meeting specifications, every time. Boards expect to harness the potential of IT to return business value. Boards want to leverage IT investments to gain better productivity and increased efficiencies. And Boards would like to be sure IT-induced risks are articulated, managed and mitigated.

The reality is that Boards are often informed of business losses, damaged reputation and weakened competitive positions stemming directly from the inappropriate application of IT. Boards are sometimes informed of IT initiatives running over budget, or over time, or of missing the strategic mark, or—worst of all—all of the above. Unintended consequences traceable to IT lead the management team to brief the Board of unmet expectations and lost productivity. And IT investments have created a new genre of risks that are now frequently the item for boardroom update—risks like worms, viruses, dynamic denial of service attacks, compromised perimeter security, cyber-threats, fated "big bang" projects, etc. In other words, Boards have been informed only when the business has been exposed to IT induced risks. It is rare for the Board to be engaged on the front-end of IT strategy setting. The case to do so is clear and compelling.

The Insightful CIO's response to this dilemma

The Insightful CIO confronts this problem head-on. He starts out by articulating a transparent environment, wherein the Board will be briefed periodically, with all news—be it good or bad. He creates easy-to-understand frameworks that can be repeatedly used in the board room.

The Insightful CIO first educates the board about how best to leverage the framework. He seeks feedback about the adequacy of the framework. He makes the needful changes to the framework, so that the end-product meets the needs of the board. To create consistency between the information shared with the Board and the information shared with the business, The Insightful CIO starts out by addressing the information needs of the business first. He then distils this information to create a Board information package. The Insightful CIO starts out by creating three categories of initiatives:

1. That "keep the lights on"; these typically relate to infrastructure services and recurring licensing needs-including issues like the dial-tone for telephony, for instance, or the web-tone for Internet services, or the

cost to renew Microsoft Office licenses, for example. One would expect that these recurring costs go down over time on a per-unit basis. However, if the business grows over time, these costs will vary, even as unit-costs may decline. These are considered to be a "cost of doing business."

2. That enhances the productivity of the enterprise and delivers ever-increasing value per IT dollar expended; typically in the transactional layers of IT—this includes cost to manage and maintain the ERP backbone of the enterprise, for instance. Declining cost-per-unit-of-delivery is the yardstick in these initiatives, as measured year on year.

3. That are geared to deliver new and differentiated value to the enterprise, be it in goods or in services. Typical examples are information provisioning to assist accelerated decision-making. Measurably increased value to the enterprise (capturing new markets, increasing overall revenue, improved customer retention and satisfaction, reduced cost of goods sold etc.) is the yardstick for such initiatives.

Next, he creates mechanisms to report on the agreed-to

objectives and progress towards their achievement. The progress of IT initiatives is of interest not only to the impacted organization but also to the broader enterprise. IT is a scarce resource and deploying IT resources is a zero-sum game to the enterprise.

The Insightful CIO creates mechanisms that ensure transparency—articulating objectives; clarifying goals; sorting initiatives into the logical stacks as set out in the previous paragraph; setting mile-stones in place; measuring progress; frequently, openly, fearlessly and in business terms, reporting on progress vs. plans. These are the fundamentals by which to create such transparency. This is an area where the CFO could collaborate with the CIO, as the former is usually better geared to collect, collate, create and distribute business score cards.

As previously discussed, with his basic feature in place, The Insightful CIO puts in place a good portfolio management framework. In many enterprises, IT initiatives progress to their logical end-state without any checks between inception and conclusion. Given today's fast-paced business environments, the base-case for an IT initiative may change before the IT solution is delivered.

He follows this step with a process that dissects all

IT initiatives and reports back status to the business. The Insightful CIO implements process frameworks that periodically reaffirm the rationale for critical initiatives, interrogate the rate of progress and status of such initiatives, and take any needful corrective actions. These are variously called phase-gate processes or "keep-or-kill" processes. Regardless of the tag given them, such process frameworks should provide the enterprise a mechanism to crisply "kill" initiatives that no longer meet the needs of the enterprise—without ascribing any value judgment on the team(s) working on such initiatives.

Reporting out is an art-form that is not easily mastered. Natural human- and organization-tendencies are to report the good news and, at least, delay the bad news. Unbiased reporting demands that all news, both good and bad, are dispassionately shared. With honesty and clarity. In fact, intellectual honesty of this caliber deserves to be recognized and rewarded.

IT-induced risks can be brushed under the carpet easily. To ensure that this does not happen, the Insightful CIO creates a mechanism to elicit risks early in the life-cycle of an initiative. Clear expectations are set in the CIO organization whereby risks are articulated with steps to measure, manage and mitigate risks.

In a fast-changing business environment with both many moving parts on a global canvas, and many new technologies, risks are not only unknown but

unknowable. To resolve this paradox, the Insightful CIO sets up mechanisms to quickly respond to new risks that have hitherto not been encountered. The Insightful CIO's goal should be to capture lessons-learned; and to disseminate these lessons quickly and effectively so that it becomes institutionalized. Rapid learning is the means to mitigate and manage the unknown.

Assessing process maturity

In the preceding section of this chapter, five different processes were articulated. Together, these processes offer a framework that adequately addresses IT governance. They are:

1. A closed-loop, cascading objectives setting and achievements process
2. A portfolio management process

3. A process to trisect the portfolio and present initiatives
4. A reporting process to create transparency
5. A comprehensive risk identification, management and mitigation process

Not all enterprises have all these processes. In fact, depending on the size of the enterprise, one or more of these processes may not be needed. This is an item for discussion between the CIO and the CEO, or even the board.

When once a set of processes is agreed upon, The Insightful CIO self-assesses the current state of maturity of these processes. Here, such maturity models as the Capability Maturity Model, or CMM, as developed by the Software Engineering Institute (SEI) in the mid-1980s can be a pragmatic way to approach measurement.

The CMM defines 6 stages to any process. They are as follows:

0.	Non-existent
1.	Initial
2.	Repeatable

3.   Defined
4.   Quantitatively managed
5.   Optimized

A Kiviat-chart (an example of which is shown here) can serve as a quick-reference to mark the initial state of the chosen processes. It can serve as a useful mechanism to track progress against a desired future state as well. It is not necessary that all IT processes are at stage 5 (Optimized). When once the Insightful CIO has self-assessed the plot-point of the current (or "as-is") state, he

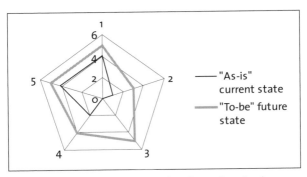

Figure 8.2 - Example Kiviat or Radar-chart, showing how a multivariate report-out to the Board could be pictorially represented

should make this a topic of discussion with the CEO. The discussion should be centered around the appropriate plot-point for each of the five processes in the envisioned (or "to-be") future.

The Insightful CIO points out to the CEO that advancing along the continuum from Stage 0 to Stage 5 is a thoughtful and deliberate process. Such a process comes with effort, time, persistence and appropriate incentives, and will need to be managed as a process improvement initiative. Investments are needed to move the needle along any of these axes. Such investments come at the expense of what may be seen as more important investments directly in IT enablement. So in essence, these are "overhead" investments in the IT function. It should be noted here that an additional investment is required to create mechanisms and processes to continuously measure and report on progress.

Reporting to the board

Should the CIO be a regular at board meetings? Not at all. However, the Insightful CIO should position a report-out of the CIO organization to the Board at least once every 6 months. Given the current state of most Boards, neither the framework for classifying processes nor the framework to measure the maturity of processes is likely to be common knowledge to directors. A healthy dialogue could start with Board education. My recommendation is the following 4-step process.

First, have the CIO describe the five fundamental processes discussed in the last couple of pages. This will serve as a good start to both Board education and a discussion with the Board. Next, have the CIO then the Board with a Kiviat chart, plotting "as-is" and "to-be" states for each of the five processes. Then, inform the Board of a plan of action to go from the "as-is" to the "to-be" state. Finally, return periodically—say, every 3 to 6 months—to update the Board on progress against plan.

Such an approach is transparent. It also gives the Board an opportunity to first become informed and then remain engaged regarding the rate of progress of IT towards its established goals.

Summary

IT governance is a process, just like any other governance. It is different only in that its lexicon is still evolving. IT appears more complex than other domains because the rate of change in this field is so high. As a result, boards are often at a loss to set the appropriate tone at the top. They are confounded by the seeming complexity and rate of change of technologies. Added to this, they are stunned by the repeated—and often, embarrassingly publicly reported - failures in IT-enabled initiatives.

A good CIO creates opportunities to dialogue with the board and keep them abreast of events and advances in his function. The Insightful CIO takes it a step further. He prepares crisp and clear frameworks to better explain the context of work delivered by his function. He leverages these models consistently and repeatedly. He openly seeks and embraces feedback, thereby creating opportunities for rich dialogues with the Board.

Agendas for discussions with the Board
A first-time agenda - Developing a relationship

1. Gist of the conversation with your CEO - Strategy alignment
2. Process framework: The 5 critical processes in IT Governance
3. Maturity framework: The 6 Stage CMM framework
4. Kiviat Chart Assessment: Where are we today? ("As-is")
5. Target: Where do we want to be? By when? ("To-be")
6. Enablers: What do we need in order to get there?
7. Re-up: When will the board get to review the CIO organization again?
8. General feedback regarding the CIO organization

A repeating agenda: Leveraging the relationship

1. Recall the Target: Where do we want to be? When?
2. Progress report: Where are we vis-à-vis the plan?
3. Corrections: If we are not on course, corrective actions planned

4. Statutory and regulatory compliance: Where are we?

5. Risk Management: Any risks that need board awareness?

6. Re-up: When will the board get to review the CIO organization again?

7. Education: Are there any specific topics of interest to the board? To learn?

8. Emerging standards and tools—An open discussion

9. Feedback for the CIO organization

Insights and probes

1. In many enterprises, CIOs are rarely, if ever, invited to join a board meeting. Do you brief the board regularly? What topics do you address?

2. CIOs do not always have a process framework to brief boards. Does your organization have a good framework that captures board-reportable processes? How similar is it to the framework proposed in this book? Would you alter your existing framework to include one or more of the processes articulated in this book?

3. Maturity models have been in use for some years now. Does your organization use any of these models? In which domain? How often do you measure maturity? How often do you share those measurements with the enterprise at large?

4. The CEO often carries key messages to the CIO from the board. Has the board articulated its desire for better alignment of IT with the business via the CEO? When? How often is this message conveyed? Has it changed over time?

5. CIOs brief CEOs regularly of key IT investments. Has your CEO communicated this to the board? When? Did you help him prepare for it? Was risk a major heading in that update package?

6. IT induces many risks to an organization on an on-going business. And as the voice of shareowners, the board has a right to be aware of such risks at all times. When was the board appraised of IT-induced risks and steps taken or underway to mitigate them?

Mental modeling for the neophyte

1. IT projects can often fail, and not always for technical reasons. How often do IT initiatives fail in your enterprise? Do they fail to come in on time? Or on budget? Or just, plain fail to deliver results? Or some combination? Which is the most frequent? Is there a common causal factor?

2. End users complaints can be a source of great insight into IT operations. Do you have a help-line for end users? Have you listened to the voice of the end user? How would you characterize the tone of voice? Satisfied and friendly? Bitter and antagonistic?

3. IT usually feels like it is under siege—with infinite demands being placed on finite resources. What is your opinion? Does IT have sufficient resources in your enterprise? Are they well aligned with the organization objectives?

4. Between keeping the lights on and providing transactional services, IT often does not have any resources left over to address information provisioning, leave alone strategic system needs.

How many resources in your CIO organization are dedicated to building strategic systems? What is the tag by which they can be recognized as dedicated to building such systems? What percentage of the IT organization is dedicated to just day-to-day maintenance and support? Do you feel that IT can be a source of competitive advantage, given the spread of resources?

9. Tilting the Playfield

"As human beings, our greatness lies not so much in being able to remake the world—that is the myth of the atomic age—as in being able to remake ourselves."

Mahatma Gandhi

The French have an expression for it. When they see someone who has that special feel about him, they call it the "Je ne sais quoi" factor. Translated roughly, it is a something that cannot be described. Some call it the X-Factor. That is the essence of greatness.

You know it when you are in the presence of greatness, just as surely as you know it when you are in the company of a donkey! Besides just the sense of it, there are certain attributes that seem to accompany greatness. At the end of the day, as William

Shakespeare says, "Be not afraid of greatness: some are born great, some achieve greatness, and some have greatness thrust upon them." In Will's observation, there is hope for all of us! The key is to be prepared for greatness—knowing what it takes, and working hard at improving the odds of achieving greatness.

What makes them great?

In my experience, great CIOs—indeed great people, in general—have had certain attributes in common. I have captured here some of the key attributes.

Great CIOs have an air of quiet confidence about them. They all project a certain wisdom that seems to speak of journeys and experiences that will support them, no matter what. My take on this attribute is that great CIOs are fundamentally explorers. They seem willing to undertake the journey not because they know the destination, but because they enjoy the journey. This is not to say that they are fool-hardy and rush headlong into uncharted territories. Instead, it is to suggest that they are willing to undertake carefully contemplated journeys, even though no one else has preceded them along that particular trail.

Great CIOs have been open in their sharing of failures. They are willing to talk about specific situations when their best laid plans went awry. I look at them in awe when they do that. It takes a great person to talk about personal failure in a public forum. It reveals the humility that seems to underpin their greatness. These great CIOs talk about what they missed in planning that led them to failure. In other words, it reveals their essential human-ness. Besides this, it also tells me that they are constantly seeking to learn. They know that continuous learning, even from failures, is the only sustainable edge.

Great CIOs have shown remarkable integrity and courage. One of them walked away from one of the most respected State CIO positions in the country, because the Legislature changed its mind about funding a key initiative to the detriment of the people in that state. Their "North Star" is ever-evident, directing their thoughts and actions, regardless of their personal situation. It tells me that they are willing to wager their all, but not their personal integrity. Their word is their bond.

Great CIOs realize that their success is never the result of just their effort alone. They are quick to point out how circumstances helped shaped success. They will tell you of the favorable alignment of the stars, of co-conspirators who helped them along the way, of lady luck smiling on them at the most unexpected of moments. To me, this has signaled that they lead with intention, after carefully assessing the circumstances. They have an intuitive feel for "the right moments" to tilt the playfield in their favor.

Great CIOs are surrounded by a great support cast. Their greatness seems to impel equivalently great talent to want to work with them, to learn from them, to be mentored by them. They are quick to attribute the success of initiatives to the great work done by their team members. It tells me that, working with such humble but great leaders, others find encouragement to dig deep and give of their best. In that, their own greatness surfaces. And so, a great team is born. Greatness begets greatness.

Great CIOs have strategic patience, a phrase that I was taught by one of my mentors. They lay down a scheme that clearly aligns itself with the need of the hour. In small, incremental steps, they show how the organization can make investments and reap benefits along virtually every step in the journey. They sell this strategy patiently, while simultaneously exhorting the enterprise to action.

Learning this from a mentor of mine, this was a ring-side seat to a Masterpiece Theater production: the vividly painted theme of the vision, the careful orchestration of scenes and events, the controlled publicity to accompany the production, and the barely-restrained anxiety of the enterprise to get started. Hello!

Great CIOs are personally committed to "the IT cause." As you may recall, this book began by referring to IT's infancy as an applied science. Much work remains to be done in better conveying the power of IT, and translating it to business benefits. Great CIOs constantly seek microphones connected to loudspeakers on podia that are powerful—to talk about how, where and when IT should be used, about why IT is a set of tools that can fundamentally change the way we understand and interact with the world. To me, this conveys their passion for their chosen field. They are evangelists at heart.

Do you have what it takes?

An open mind. Integrity. Courage. A willingness to explore. To fail, but to learn from failure, or "fail-forward", as it is often called. An intuitive ability to read the tea-leaves. An aura that attracts the best talent to want to work with you. Strategic patience. Personal commitment. Oratory capability. Humility. Humor. These are the words and phrases that—somewhat incompletely—describe the attributes of a great CIO.

We are all different. Many of us are born with a few of these attributes. And a few of us have many of these attributes. Some of these attributes are innate. They are expressed naturally in our interactions. Others are learned and learn-able. Good coaches and mentors can help in developing those attributes.

The fact that you have invested time in reading this book says that you are committed to personal improvement. That is a necessary condition to achieving greatness. In my experience, good mentoring has been invaluable as an additional ingredient. It is difficult to assess oneself with objectivity. Having a trusted advisor to do so can be powerful, useful, and perhaps even painful. The results, however, will likely exceed your expectations.

So how can YOU achieve greatness?

My suggestion is two-fold. First, think of great people whom you admire, regardless of their domain of expertise or the time-period in history when they achieved greatness. Perhaps you have one such idol; perhaps many. They may have been a relative, a friend, a teacher perhaps. Or a world renowned politician, statesman, musician. It does not matter. What made them great to you? Make a list of attributes that captured your heart and mind. Then, assemble your personal Board of Advisors.

Mythology tells us that Ulysses knew the value of having a guide, an objective teacher, for his son. His son's name, we are told, was Telemachus. So he requested Mentor to guide Telemachus' development while he attended to his tasks. That ancient method was practiced in many parts of the world and continues to be effective today.

So find your Mentor. Better yet, assemble a group of mentors—your own Board of Advisors. Be sure that they understand your desire for self-improvement. Share with them the list of attributes you have assembled. In course of your interactions with them, periodically request them to judge you on the attributes that you have listed.

Do you see improvement? Blind-spots? What are you doing to shed light on them? Do you have a schedule to show improvement? How do you plan to measure and report progress?

The journey to greatness begins with a brutally candid assessment. It is followed by an enthusiastic and courageous journey into the as-yet unknown. The journey can appear tedious and discouraging. A few persevering souls improve themselves. Over time, others point to them and ask, "What makes these people so different?"

Like all good things in life, greatness is a scarce commodity. And like all good things in life, it is the pursuit, and not the achievement, that makes it worth all the effort.

Good luck and God speed in your journey!

...And With A Little Help From My Friends

"It takes a village to raise a child." So goes an old African proverb. Writing books is not dissimilar. The author is often no more than the instrument writing the book, especially so for the first-time author. It is those others who are the real "authors" - the friends and family that egged on the novice-author, vetted his ideas, and supported him with encouragement as he authored the book..

This is my story of becoming an author.

Rajesh ("Raj") Setty is an engaging and interesting person. He is a successful serial entrepreneur—passionate and articulate when talking about his latest idea or business. But when he talks about reading, listening and learning, his eyes really light up.

I was introduced to Raj by a mutual friend—Karthik

Sundaram. Karthik is a consummate connector (and, incidentally, the ruthless editor for this book.) His prolific network in the tech sector is the result of many years of work leading Silicon India, a Silicon Valley magazine that focuses on the professional ranks of the Indian diaspora globally, with a special focus on Indians and technology in the Valley. I still remember the day Karthik introduced me to Raj. I was a newbie in Silicon Valley. Karthik wanted me to get plugged-in. He invited several of his friends to drinks and dinner at a swank restaurant in Palo Alto. I was carrying a new MP3 player—an exclusive offering from walmart.com, my place of employ at the time. The MP3 player looked like an ice cube; and served as a perfect ice-breaker between strangers meeting for the first time. Raj was quite taken with the device. And as we started talking, it soon became clear that he and I both traced our roots to Bangalore in India. Suddenly, the world shrank!

A few days later, I met Raj again. This time, it was at an event where I was sharing my story, so to speak, with an audience invited by SIPA (Silicon Valley Indian Professionals Association.) Raj was there —to listen and learn, as he later put it to me. Following the story-telling session, SIPA invited me to join their Board of Advisors. I accepted. When I showed up at the next meeting, Raj was there too—it turns out that we would be fellow-Advisors to SIPA.

Over the next 2 years, our paths crossed many times. We discovered many mutual zones of interest—one of them being learning as a life-long pursuit. Raj is a prolific author—he has over a dozen books to his credit—and a voracious reader. I like to read too. It is in this area that we found ourselves to be kindred souls. Raj started to push me quite early in our relationship to think of writing a book. His thought was that there were many books focused on leadership, books on IT and IT strategy, books on technology and hundreds of books on management. But there were no books on how to be an Insightful CIO. Raj pushed me hard over the following months to consider writing such a book—even if it meant using a ghost-writer to do so. He even offered to call me 10-15 times for 30 minute conversations when he, himself, would record the conversations and help frame the book!

Raj's infectious enthusiasm started to rub-off on me. It is the case that I enjoy teaching. Over the years, I have lectured at a variety of institutions—from the Chapman University in Orange, CA, the University of California, Irvine, the UCLA and UC Berkeley. My talks have almost invariably addressed topics related to Information

Technology strategies and approaches. While shortage of time had not permitted me to consider writing such a book, a framework for an interesting book had started to form in my mind. Then, in the winter of 2006/2007, I found myself with time when I stepped down as General Manager and CIO for Wal-Mart global.com.

It is easy to become convinced of your own passion! So I decided to reach out to another dear friend who is intimately involved with CIOs for validation. Robert ("Bob") Dethlefs is CEO of Evanta Inc., a company that was recently acquired by DMG. Bob's business strategy with Evanta was to cater brilliantly-focused offerings to the CIO community. Over the years, Evanta staged both CIO Executive Summits and co-sponsored the CIO Institute in such institutions as UC Berkeley, UCLA and Columbia.

Bob is a very thoughtful person. After mulling over my proposal for a couple of days, he replied with a strong vote to move forward. Later, when I reached out to Bob to ask if he could help me with publicity, his answer was not a simple "yes," as I had expected. Instead, right in the course of our conversation, Bob created an entire multi-step plan!

Over the years, one of my mentors has drilled into me that "luck is what happens when preparation meets opportunity."

Seneca, the Roman dramatist, is attributed that quote.

I suddenly found myself being presented with an opportunity—an opportunity to start writing this book. My first ever attempt at writing anything more than a detailed letter! In retrospect, I must say that this was both a longer journey than I first anticipated; and a more enjoyable one than the one I had imagined.

Thank you, Karthik, Raj and Bob, for pushing me and encouraging me to commit my thoughts to paper. Preparing this manuscript for possible publication has been a fantastic journey.

I am blessed with good friends and well-wishers.

I feel lucky!

Ashwin Rangan